ILLUSTRATIONS

CHARLES F. C. LADD, JR.	*Frontispiece*

FACING PAGE

FACULTY GROUP	32
THE DIABUTSU OF KAMAKURA	90
BOOMING THE BIG BELL OF NARA	128
AUDIENCE GIVEN BY THE KING AND QUEEN OF SIAM	166
THE TAJ MAHAL	204
WITH THE SULTAN OF LAHEJ—ARABIA	212
RECEPTION BY MUSSOLINI AT CHIGI PALACE	262

AROUND THE WORLD
AT SEVENTEEN

AROUND THE WORLD AT SEVENTEEN

By
CHARLES F. C. LADD, Jr.

PUBLISHED BY
QUINN & BODEN COMPANY, INC.
RAHWAY, N. J.

Copyright, 1928, by
CHARLES F. C. LADD

CHARLES F. C. LADD, JR.

*Dedicated
To My Father*

CHAPTER ONE

THE first paragraph of a news item in the *New York World,* dated September 19, 1926, reads: "Globe Trot College set sail from Hoboken at 4 p.m. yesterday, on its first semester of eight months with the world for its curriculum."

On the night of September 17, the spacious Waldorf Astoria Hotel played host to a gathering unique in its long and eventful history. Fifteen hundred people crowded its galleries and ballroom. People from every state in the Union were there, a select group representing the best citizenship in hundreds of American communities. It was not a bankers' reception, although many bankers and their wives, sons and daughters, were present. Wealth and power and culture and good breeding were observable everywhere. There were dancing and speech-making and dining. An undercurrent of excitement and anticipation was reflected in the subdued laughter and hum of voices. Five hundred picked American boys and girls, every one a modern Ulysses, were preparing to embark on the most remarkable voyage of modern times—the around the world cruise of the first "floating university."

For fifty years, in this country, such an institution

Around the World at Seventeen

was discussed, but it was Dean James E. Lough, Professor of Psychology in the University of New York, who made the idea a reality. Other universities of the country sponsored the movement, agreeing to allow credits for all work done on board the ship. The *Ryndam,* a vessel of the Holland-American Line, was chartered, and call for enrollments sent out, which resulted in one hundred thirty women and three hundred sixty-four men, totaling four hundred ninety-four students, signing up for the eight months' cruise.

Mother and I attended the reception at the Waldorf, where I met a number of friends. There were fourteen of us from Kansas City. Our first glimpse of the boat came the day after the reception, September 18, just a few hours before we were scheduled to sail.

Before I go further with the recountal of my experiences aboard the University Afloat, I wish emphatically to state that, from an educational standpoint, the cruise was a success. I would be indeed unappreciative of the benefits I derived from my eight months aboard the *Ryndam,* if I purposely made statements that misled my readers into believing anything to the contrary. At the beginning of any new enterprise mistakes occur, misunderstandings arise, and confusion often reigns, all of which are reduced to a minimum under wise leadership.

Around the World at Seventeen

Furthermore, this is a good time to explain that I passed all my courses with creditable grades; in fact I made better grades than I had ever made on land. I can account for this only by explaining that the cruise was divided forty per cent on the sea and sixty per cent in ports. Naturally, there was no studying done while sightseeing, but while on the "bounding main" there was little else to do.

When Mother and I visited the *Ryndam*, we found the vessel rather small to accommodate comfortably the eight hundred souls aboard. I was one among the last to join the cruise, and ex-governor Henry J. Allen, of Kansas, who was a member of the "floating" faculty secured accommodations for me. Of course, as a late comer, I could not expect the best. But when we groped our way down to my assigned quarters on deck C, the polite designation for the steerage, Mother and I looked at each other in dismay. For a moment my destiny almost took another course; a word spoken, and the world would have been deprived of this literary gem.

Trifling incidents, however, sometimes shape big events. Mother overheard a girl complaining of her quarters on deck A, by far the best on the boat aside from those occupied by faculty members and their wives. The girl's unreasonableness struck us as absurd. After all, it was a question of view-point. At any rate, the incident saved the day; and the big

Around the World at Seventeen

event of my trip around the world was, you might say, signed, sealed, and delivered on the spot.

The depression I momentarily felt on viewing my cabin was swept away in the excitement of leave-taking. After two hours of confusion, of the barking of taxi-cab klaxons, of the rumble of trucks, of farewells and embraces and hand clasps, the gangplank was hauled aboard, the sturdy little tugs set up a great pounding and spluttering and we were slowly pulled and pushed into the ship channel of the North River.

As the *Ryndam* widened the distance between its starboard side and the dock, fore and aft, in fo'c'stle glory hole, galley and poop-deck, faces smiled a little wistfully from portholes and railings across the ever-widening strip of water, at the thousand-odd spectators on the dock. Handkerchiefs, hats, and arms were waved in farewell to friends and relatives. Tears misted the eye and not a little doubt weighed the heart, as our prow turned oceanward, and the first "floating university" began its first around the world cruise.

Mother later told me the ship looked very impressive with the scores of colored flags flying from every halyard, and the ship's sides inscribed with the large white letters, "University World Cruise," while the strains of the Dutch band aboard ship grew fainter and fainter as the distance separated us.

Around the World at Seventeen

According to the schedule, we were to spend one hundred and six days on shore and one hundred and nineteen days on board the *Ryndam,* doing a year of regular university work in a little more than half the time allotted by universities on land.

But of more importance than the mere matter of routine class-room work was the responsibility the thinking student felt toward his country. We were the most representative group of men and women who ever left the shores of America to travel in foreign lands. Everywhere, the United States as a nation would be judged by our manner and deportment. We were emissaries of good-will and it rested in our power to strengthen the existing friendly relations between our nation and the ones we visited, or to create a feeling of aversion and hostility to American ideas and ideals.

As we rounded the *Ambrose* lightship, the sturdy little tugs cast off and we were "on our own." Already I had formed my own ideas about living on a ship. We glided so smoothly, so majestically away from the dock, that I felt a new sense of content at the *Ryndam's* easy riding qualities. No matter what happened, there would be no flat tires to fix, and no bumps. One thing only caused me anxiety; was I to be, or not to be, seasick? With this constantly in my mind, I very carefully selected my food at meals, and held my breath in suspense. But the second day

Around the World at Seventeen

out I was convinced I had got my sea-legs, and for me there was to be no seasickness.

Matriculation and scheduling of courses required considerable time the first four or five days. Until I trod the deck of the *Ryndam* I did not know the port side from the starboard, and had no reason for doubting the forward hatch was a place where chickens came into the world. So I spent part of the time acquiring a knowledge of sea terms; part of the time getting acquainted, and the remainder of the time studying.

On the second day out we were assigned to our life-boats, thirty persons to the group. If I recall rightly mine was No. 15, not being quite sure as I saw the boat only once again. We were told that any time we heard three blasts from the engine whistle we were to congregate beside our particular boat. On the third afternoon out, the alarm sounded and all rushed on deck to their stations. It so happened, my boat contained only boys. This occasioned unpleasant remarks that brought about the officials changing ten girls to our group. These boats were equipped with kegs of fresh water, hardtack rations, and a supply of oil, the latter to be used to calm the waves about the boat.

I spent considerable time in the prow of the ship, watching the ocean. The second day out came the first test of seasickness. We had just missed a terrific

Around the World at Seventeen

storm off Cape Hatteras, and there was a heavy ocean swell. I stood the test without a qualm, but seventy-five others were quite ill. The meals, particularly breakfast, proved disappointing. The Dutch had their own ideas about our eating and at five minutes to nine every morning the doors of the dining-room closed. A drug store sandwich and cold-drink counter, or a hot-dog stand, would have made a fortune on the *Ryndam*.

After four days at sea, an entry in my log book sums up my first impressions of ocean travel. It reads: "I am feeling a little anxious to get into port, to see and touch familiar things. A street-car would be a not unwelcome sight."

CHAPTER TWO

HAVANA at last! At six o'clock on the morning of September 23, the *Ryndam* docked at a long, white pier, much more modern than the one at which we embarked at New York. We were greeted by five hundred shouting, gesticulating, good-natured Cubans who seemed really interested in the American Floating University.

Havana was our first foreign port and I had no idea what it would be like, unless it bore a resemblance to our border towns because of the common Spanish blood. I had hoped we would dock late enough on entering the bottle-neck harbor to get a view of the famous, or perhaps infamous, El Moro castle, about which so many blood-thirsty tales cluster.

I was one of the first off the boat and was herded in a group past Cuban customs officers who were more resplendent in their uniforms than any "admiral" manning the doorway in a fashionable New York hotel. These individuals eyed us hard and suspiciously, but presently we were freed and we made our way to the sidewalk, where one hundred cars waited to convey us on a number of prearranged excursions. Let it be known they were real automo-

Around the World at Seventeen

biles. I drew a sport model Cadillac and the seat beside the driver.

Ever since we left New York I had anticipated trying out my border Spanish in Havana. Under the chauffeur's guise the Spanish of our driver was plain to see. He looked like a cross between King Alfonso, Porfierio Diaz, and a Cuban *revolucionario*. I cleared my throat and shot a question at him in his own beloved Spanish. He looked at me blankly. I reiterated the question. His answer was discouraging—at least to my linguistic attempt. He said with a Boweryesque accent, "Wat ya tink dis is? Be yerself, mister!"

To get back to the excursion: The student body was divided into sections A, B, C, etc., and with whatever section you were assigned, you were supposed to remain. But any one with the least feeling of independence followed his own conscience in the matter. For my part, if I were with one group and I saw that another had better automobiles, better accommodations, or more interesting attractions, I hied myself thither.

But no matter what section you were in, Havana was well worth seeing. I found the down-town section consisted mainly of two kinds of streets. In the older and more congested quarter a flagpole sprang from nearly every building and occasional awnings hung futilely over narrow sidewalks cluttered with

Around the World at Seventeen

a display of all sorts of merchandise. The streets, especially where street-cars had invaded these ancient precincts, barely allowed room for an automobile to pass between curb and track. Other streets were yet narrower and cars passed each other with difficulty. It was customary, nevertheless, for them to dash along at a speed of twenty-five to fifty miles an hour, in much the breath-taking fashion of taxi-cab drivers in Paris. Nobody pays any attention to the nine-mile law. They say it has been a dead letter since it was adopted twenty years ago but, as Cuba is a land where no one wishes to do extra work, it is too much trouble to change it.

The buildings in the main were built of symmetrically hewn, white rock, two, three and sometimes four stories high. Set in this continental atmosphere, electric signs lend an incongruous, modernistic note to the effect. On the other hand, the later-built business sections have amply wide streets, paved, clean, and as smooth as the best in our country. The buildings, not high and of rather massive architecture, front the sidewalks with stone columns extending over shady recesses in which the pedestrians can escape the tropical sun.

After viewing the business sections, we drove out on the Prado, which is the street of streets in Havana, broad, paved, and tree-lined. It has been said that this is the most beautiful ocean drive in the world

Around the World at Seventeen

and while I question the statement, the view of the sea and the cool breezes on the hot day, were both pleasing to the eye and to one's comfort.

We drove along some distance to a monument erected to eight native students assassinated for plotting against the Spanish tyrants of the old régime. Leaving the Prado, we drove into the residential district. There were not many Spanish type homes; strangely enough there were more on the order of English country places, and Dutch architecture was much in evidence. The latter type was reminiscent of those hardy Dutch voyagers who played a prominent part in exploiting the resources of the Latin-American countries. Altogether, one suspects that the beautiful homes were constructed by Americans of these prohibition days, who love to play in the land of the mint-julep.

We next drove past the Country Club which resembles many of our own, and on to the Tropical Botanical Gardens, owned by the Havana brewery. Every imaginable sort of shrub and plant is to be found in these wonderful gardens but the interest of everybody seemed to be centered on a large sign which read, "Free beer, this way." Whereupon the crowd made a rush for the beverage of interest. Unfortunately, I was "caught on the rail" and was crowded out at the finish, failing even to sample the famous draught.

Around the World at Seventeen

Incidentally, the trip to the Botanical Gardens when first discussed caused considerable worry to certain faculty members. It was to be our initial test of discipline and self-control. Here was a situation that threw a whole college into a beer garden where beer was free.

"The cruise is doomed," groaned one professor; "these boys will never get over it!"

"Wait till we see the results," said sensible Dean Heckel, the member in charge of discipline. "Surely you do not think the cruise can go around the world without the students discovering the existence of beer!"

According to the general impression which prevailed in Havana, Americans were one hundred per cent wet; and no doubt Havana and the faculty, as well, were surprised when the student body returned to the boat with only four or five of its members showing the least evidence of the visit to the—shall we say, Botanical Gardens?

Our next stop was at the Colon cemetery, one of the most ancient burial grounds. If one in the busy workaday world had time to ruminate on incongruous subjects, perhaps none would hold more interest than five hundred curious, red-blooded, young American students, up to date to their very finger tips, viewing the "shades of the departed," while a professional "spieler" stood amid the tombstones and

Around the World at Seventeen

vociferated into a megaphone on the virtues, the bravery, the self-sacrifice of the aforementioned eight revolting native students who lay buried beneath the tomb on which he whacked with his cane. Add to this the sirens, klaxons, and horns that shrieked and buzzed and screamed—a medley of sounds executed in the best technic of one hundred picked Havana chauffeurs—and you can easily picture our trip to the cemetery. Then we all went to lunch.

The afternoon was free for independent action and a party of us consisting of five boys and three girls started in search of Sloppy Joe's, a place famous for its pineapple drink. In the proprietor, we found a most amusing character. On learning we were a bunch from the floating university in search of his famous beverage, he hospitably exclaimed, "Let it be known that Sloppy Joe gives the first pineapple drink to the first students of the first floating university!" While we were at Sloppy Joe's, the Mayor of Havana came in, although I did not know until later that he was there. The last friendly act of Sloppy Joe was to direct our crowd to a good place to eat, which was vastly more important to us than beholding a mayor.

It was a little restaurant in the same block as his, to which Sloppy Joe sent us, with plenty of atmosphere, typically Cuban, I judged. Despite the failure of my linguistic effort on our driver, I wanted to try

Around the World at Seventeen

ordering a meal in Spanish. So I called first for *tortillas*, and was gratified to see that the waiter clearly understood me. After a few minutes, he came back beaming—with a ham omelette! The Latin races are the most obliging and courteous in the world. If you are driving, for instance, and wish to know the distance from one point to another and ask, "How far is it to the dock, ten blocks?" The Latin will obligingly reply, "*Sí, señor.*" Although, as a matter of fact, it may be twenty blocks or twenty miles. So when the waiter returned with a ham omelette, I naturally inferred that he did not understand my order. I patiently explained that a *tortilla* was round and flat and otherwise described what we Americans would call a pancake. The waiter smiled enthusiastically and returned to the kitchen. I sat back confident that at last I had made my order known. Presently, he came back with a plain omelette. I began to suspect something was wrong with my Spanish but my spirits were somewhat restored when I learned that in Cuba *tortilla* means omelette. I also learned that *chili con carne* and *enchiladas* were unknown to the waiter; but he was familiar enough with Lobster Newburg. Beyond a doubt, world travel broadens one's knowledge of things.

After the meal Paul Robinson and I went in search of postcards, while the others returned to the boat.

Before we had left the boat, the captain issued an

Around the World at Seventeen

edict, suggestion and warning, all in one, to the effect that the *Ryndam* sailed from Havana harbor at five o'clock sharp. He volunteered the further information that a boat sailed for New Orleans and a train ran from there to Los Angeles in forty-eight hours, and the fare by that route was $290. For reasons I need not explain, no student cared to incur the additional expense, much less lose four thousand-odd miles of the cruise. So it behooved everybody to keep their eye on the sailing time.

Paul and I became so engrossed in our post-card mailing, however, that the time slipped by, and when I looked at my watch it was already past five. With a yell of warning to Paul, I dashed out of the shop and into the dirty, narrow street, elbowing the leisurely natives who no doubt thought there was a new revolution brewing. I formed perfect interference for Paul, and we continued in this wise until we dashed through the dock buildings and onto the wharf.

The gang-plank was already withdrawn and the *Ryndam*, inch by inch, was pulling away from the dock. I made a leap for a swinging rope ladder, with Paul at my elbow, and we both managed to secure a hold on the lowest rung just as the ladder was being hauled over the rail. It was a close call, but we made it down to our steerage boudoir undetected, and there panted out our congratulations to each other.

In retrospect, my first experience in a foreign port

Around the World at Seventeen

was not unpleasant. Despite its dirt and squalor on one hand, and its modernity on the other, Havana lays hold of the imagination. One recalls that on October 28, 1492, Columbus limped into the bottleneck harbor, planted the flag of Spain on the virgin shore and claimed the country for Queen Isabella. These same shores later knew the black flags of the pirates, Morgan, Kidd and Blackbeard. Again, from this harbor, Hernando de Soto, the governor of Cuba, in 1538, followed the trail of Ponce de León to conquer Florida, to discover the Mississippi and to meet his death after months of wandering over the new land. The flags of six nations have flown in the breeze of this sunny country. Twice in the sixteenth century, French fleets destroyed the town. In 1628, Dutch buccaneers captured it. The British took possession in 1762, but later restored it to Spain; and during the Spanish-American war, our own Stars and Stripes floated on the halyards of the flagpoles. To-day, the flag of the Republic of Cuba floats proudly over its capital city of a half-million people.

Near the wharf where the *Ryndam* docked is the Plaza de Armas, which marks the spot where Havana was founded in 1519. On one side stands the somber and crumbling fortress, La Fuerta, built in 1538 by de Soto. Another point of interest is the Cathedral of the Virgin Mary of the Immaculate Conception. The story runs that the bones of Columbus were

Around the World at Seventeen

brought here from Santo Domingo when that island was captured by the French in 1795, and there they remained until the Spaniards were driven from Cuba in 1898, when they transported them to their final resting place in the Cathedral of Seville.

Another point of interest in Havana is the Students' Monument, a panel set in the wall of the former Spanish Commissary Building, the grounds of which were used for public executions. There, in 1871, the eight revolting students, the eldest of whom was only sixteen, were shot. Forty students were implicated in the plot, growing out of a duel between a young Cuban and a Spanish journalist, in which the latter was killed. After the execution of the eight, an investigation in Spain resulted in the entire forty being declared innocent—a fair illustration of ironic justice.

The entrance to the Colon cemetery, at Havana, which the entire cruise visited, is gained through a great arch with treble gates. Over the central gate a group of figures represent Columbus bringing the light of religion to the new world. Near the center of the burial ground stands the tomb of General Gomez, chief of the Cuban army insurrection. Burials are made in crevices hewn from solid rock and the graves are covered with marble slabs. These niches are rented for a term of years. If for any reason the relatives of the deceased make no further

Around the World at Seventeen

payments, the bones are removed to the Bone House, a massive walled structure, about seventy-five feet square by fifty feet deep.

After we steamed out of the harbor of Havana on our way to Panama, we encountered our first rough sea. All movable objects were lashed down. Almost every one suffered from sea-sickness. But I was more fortunate.

To observe more closely my first storm at sea, I donned my slicker, sou'wester, and rubber boots and made my way to the prow of the boat. It was an almost untenable position, the constant pressure of the wind forcing me to entwine myself around a capstan, while the nose-dives of the boat into the trough of the mountainous sea created a sensation one may feel in descending on an express elevator in the Woolworth building. After the boat reached the bottom of the trough, it met me coming back. There is something magnificent as well as awe-inspiring in the fury of the storm at sea, but I had had enough and I retreated on my hands and knees to a safer position where I could watch the storm in greater comfort and security.

CHAPTER THREE

AFTER three days, uneventful save for the one storm, at eleven a.m., September 27, we arrived at Colon, the Atlantic entrance to the Panama Canal and an important coaling station. Colon was more cosmopolitan but less continental than Havana. This difference is noticeable, both in the foreign races one meets and in the physical appearance of the town. The buildings are more like those seen in the Orient, railed-in verandas, two and three stories high, fronting the streets, while here and there a gallery juts, or a bright-colored portico heightens the "ginger-bread" effect. The colors of the buildings are more somber —the dull maroon backgrounds often enlivened by bright yellow balustrades inclosing the veranda. This holds good particularly of the Calle Bolivar, one of the main thoroughfares of Colon. One's impression of the town is similar to that gained on beholding a derelict, after long exposure to the sea.

The white races are in the minority and most of the merchandising is carried on by Hindu, Japanese, and Chinese venders, who can see an American coming half a mile away. The natives are very poor and I noticed them in the marketplaces buying parts of fish for fractions of a cent.

Around the World at Seventeen

Paul Robinson was with me when I made my first foreign purchase—a Japanese kimono for Mother. The vender, a Hindu, insisted on eighteen dollars for it. A ten dollar bill was all I had with me and I did not intend to return to the boat for more money. Anyway, eighteen dollars was too much to ask for the garment; so after considerable haggling, he gave it to me for the ten spot and my note for the remaining eight dollars. He still has the note. At that, I am sure he knows he got the best of the trade. Later, in Japan I could have purchased a finer garment for two or three dollars.

Robinson had his movie camera with him and we tried it out on a *cochero,* old as Methuselah, bewhiskered and dirtily picturesque, who drove us through the narrow streets, the wheels of his *coche* clattering on the cobblestones that were laid perhaps before he was born.

We lunched at the Washington Hotel, a magnificent hostelry surrounded by beautiful gardens with palm trees shading the grounds; and afterwards we attended an aquatic meet, in which many notable swimmers participated but none of the students.

The next morning at six o'clock, the vessel having coaled and taken on six hundred and seventy tons of fresh water, we began our journey through the Panama Canal.

The canal was a disappointment to me. Its great-

Around the World at Seventeen

ness can be estimated only by its intrinsic value to the world's shipping progress. When it is seen from a boat, its operation might be likened to pulling the stopper out of a bathtub and filling it again. Contrary to the general conception, in passing from the Atlantic to the Pacific, the direction of the canal is southeast, in length it is 43.84 nautical miles. Here is a case where literally the Pacific is *east* of the Atlantic; also the Atlantic Ocean is about ten feet higher in elevation than the Pacific. Three series of locks take the vessel to Gatun Lake. The lake is dotted with little islands covered with jungle growth of bambo trees and small date palms. I took up a position in the prow, next to the pilot house, perhaps, the best point for observation on the boat.

On the day we passed through, there was no ocean breeze to temper the torrid heat. On each side the tall cliffs crowded down, smothering us by their nearness. Passing out of Gatun Lake, we descended through another series of locks to Balboa, the Pacific entrance of the canal.

The seaport, Balboa, bears the same relation to Panama City as San Pedro harbor does to Los Angeles, being a more modern part of the old city. It is the largest and most interesting town in Panama, with a number of picturesque parks and an historical atmosphere. It was at this point the stout adventurer, Vasco Núñez de Balboa, in 1513, first saw the Pacific.

Around the World at Seventeen

The usual hundred automobiles met us at the dock and we drove through the dirty streets of old Panama City, past gray, moss-covered churches, on to the golf course. On the way, we passed a group of men in uniforms of our gobs breaking rocks with sledge-hammers—in the vernacular, "making little ones out of big ones." One of them hailed us, grinning through the rivulets of perspiration that streamed down his face, "Hello, boys, join the navy and see the world!" Then he swung his hammer viciously at a rock.

We drove to a high promontory from which we glimpsed the real Pacific beyond the scattered rocky islands. Somewhere beyond the lesser ones lies Pearl Island, famous for the fineness of the gems for which it was named. Below the promontory, a mob of dirty urchins yelled up at us, and in reply we threw pennies among them and watched the scramble after the coins. It was just another method of earning a living. We lunched and returned to the boat in time to sail at five o'clock.

I suppose it is customary for every traveler-writer to bore his readers with descriptions of Nature as seen in different climes. No words can picture adequately the beauty of a tropical sunset with the ocean beneath, placid, as if it were preparing for sleep, and clouds massed low in the west like frowning warriors on guard, while the cloud-banks turn from ruby red,

Around the World at Seventeen

to lavender, to slate-gray, then gradually fade into far mountains of snowy whiteness. By that time the sun had dipped beneath the ocean, tropic twilight had stolen over the earth, the phosphorescent fish illumined the quiet water with dull green light, and the star-sprinkled heavens canopied the silence. Night had come.

Believe me when I say we needed all the inspiration that a benign Nature bestowed upon us in amelioration of the strange conditions in which we found ourselves. The revolt of modern youth is nothing compared with mine on trying to adjust myself to my steerage "boudoir." William S. Worthington, of Salt Lake City, whom I fortunately drew as roommate, shared my sentiments. Put a chap almost six feet and rather slender, which describes me, with another chap who measures about five feet high by four broad, which identifies Worthington, into steerage quarters five by nine by seven, and something interesting is bound to happen. When the *Ryndam* was built, the Dutch evidently had not reached their growth and the first week or two I spent experimenting in ways and means to accommodate my length to that of my berth. It became a game with me to keep six inches from sticking out somewhere. Worthington, built more along Dutch lines, was deprived of the pastime. But I more than evened up when in dressing for "parade" he was forced to go into the

Around the World at Seventeen

passageway to put on his coat. So much for the size of our living quarters. We had one porthole just under a bilge pipe, and when the wind was in the wrong direction we were compelled to keep it closed to exclude the pungent odors and waste waters from the ship. There was only a thin metal bulkhead, or partition, between us and the coal-bunkers. At all hours of the night and day we could hear the firemen with their shovels and sledge-hammers, a racket sometimes varied by the scraping of slack coal sliding down the chutes. All of these were pleasant sounds and great aids to concentration. To add to our discomfort, coal dust in some unaccountable manner sifted through onto our bedding and clothes, coloring them black as ink. Yet, as I look back now, these discomforts were of minor importance—just those conditions all pioneers face cheerfully and overcome. If one expects only luxury, then one should not pioneer.

Worthington and I decorated our quarters in true college style. We sneaked into the hold where the carpenters' supplies were kept and "borrowed" hammer and nails and lumber with which we built a study desk. Then we tacked up a map of the world and kept account of the ship's progress by means of pins stuck in the dots representing the various ports of call. With the temperature generally hovering around a hundred degrees, the privacy

Around the World at Seventeen

of our deck was a godsend, for it permitted us to wear abbreviated clothing. Apropos of wearing apparel, with the exception of our sojourn in China and Japan, we wore white linen throughout the voyage until after we left Cairo.

One could almost tell in what section of the boat lived the groups from the various states. In the passageway near the quarters of the boys from New York, for instance, street signs marked off Broadway. Twelfth Street indicated the quarters of the Kansas City fellows, and it may be of interest to know that street signs of the Middle West towns predominated, indicating the student body was recruited largely from that section.

The routine of the trip from Balboa to San Pedro, the harbor of Los Angeles, was uneventful, save for two incidents. The Planet Players gave their first play of the cruise, in the assembly room which, however, was so crowded that many of us were forced to resort to the small boys' favorite method at ball games—only instead of peering through knotholes, we hung head downward in the hatches.

The second incident, however, gave everybody quite a thrill. Just before reaching San Pedro harbor we encountered the Pacific battle fleet at target practice, the huge battleships belching great columns of black smoke, followed by deafening roars, as they hurled their leaden missiles at the floating targets.

Around the World at Seventeen

The commander of the battle fleet radioed a warning to our boat to stay out of the line of fire; but the *Ryndam* held her course, which gave us a splendid view of our great fleet in action. Suppose, however, a gunner in calculating the elevation of a shot had misjudged the roll of his ship, and fired with the dip of the vessel? I do not think the hull of the *Ryndam* was built to withstand a leaden pill of a ton or so fired at her from short range. But our gunners are as good as the best; our ship steamed serenely through the gauntlet untouched; and while we were still speculating on what might have happened *IF*—we docked at a commodious pier in San Pedro.

After a rigid custom inspection those of us who asked for the privilege were turned loose. A large group greeted us at the dock and while for me, there were no familiar faces present, relatives and friends of many students had crossed the continent to visit once more with those who soon would be out of American waters until, seven months later, we should again drop anchor in New York harbor.

Dessa Skinner and I hired a taxi-cab to drive the twenty-five miles to Los Angeles. Dessa already had a room engaged at the Biltmore Hotel and had invited me to share it with him. After seemingly interminable days on shipboard, we both craved luxury.

Registering at the Biltmore, we ordered the best meal money could buy, and you can imagine how we

Around the World at Seventeen

stretched our legs in comfortable chairs and ordered the bell-boys around. As I was already familiar with Los Angeles I went on none of the cruise excursions to Hollywood, the beaches, and the other sight-seeing rounds.

Instead of those activities Skinner and I decided to make our first aeroplane flight. We taxied out to the flying field and for the price of eight dollars apiece the pilot agreed to take us on a hundred-mile flight. I considered myself a "veteran," due to an experience Father and I once had in a two-seater which because of our combined over-weight refused to do more than barely hop off the ground and light again. But at that I got a great "kick" out of the flight. We flew first over San Pedro harbor, sighting the *Ryndam*, down to the Catalina Islands, and out to sea twenty miles, where the land was barely discernible in a dim haze. From there we flew back over the mountains and Los Angeles, making altogether a trip of an hour and a half. We had on our white linen suits and the cold was terrific. After alighting, the only way we could express our appreciation of the flight was in the sign language; we were stone deaf for two hours.

Of course, while in Los Angeles we dined at Victor Hugo's, where the famous dish is a three-foot pone of bread placed in a glass in the center of the table. When you wanted a slice you twisted it off.

One of the first things I did was to talk to Mother

Around the World at Seventeen

and Father in San Antonio by telephone. Altogether, I had a much more strenuous time in Los Angeles than I had planned, what with midnight lunches, taking in the movies, and talking about good old Kansas City. The next morning we took advantage of our opportunity to sleep late, then spent the remainder of the day—we were scheduled to sail in the evening—scouting for provisions to take with us.

We bought a large stalk of green bananas and other green fruit, to ripen on the voyage to the Hawaiian Islands, a quantity of apples, a large brick of cheese, and two big boxes of graham crackers, besides an assortment of candy. As a farewell plunge into luxury at Los Angeles, we had our dinner, wherein every favorite dish was included, served in our room at the Biltmore. Then we checked out, loaded our provisions into a seven-passenger Packard limousine, bade *adios* to Los Angeles, and drove to the boat. It took three stewards to carry our supplies to our quarters which was accomplished in time for us to sail at seven o'clock for Hawaii.

CHAPTER FOUR

ONCE again on shipboard, every one's attention turned back to classroom work, which, by this time, was well under way and progressing satisfactorily. One of my studies was French, in which language I hoped to gain moderate proficiency by the time we reached the Mediterranean, so I could at least order a dinner without being embarrassed. While English is becoming more prevalent in foreign countries, French, as yet, is the *lingua franca* at the cross roads of the world.

When we steamed out of San Pedro harbor, the ship's log indicated 5,638 miles from New York. Practically one-sixth of the distance was put behind us in less than one-eighth of the calendar length of the cruise.

I suppose it was as difficult for the Dutch crew to become accustomed to the American ways as it was for us to become accustomed to theirs. Very likely they discussed and criticized our manners among themselves. But there was this difference in viewpoint: they were getting paid for their work, while we were paying for ours. Therefore, I feel free to speak my mind. Very often we up-and-coming

Around the World at Seventeen

Americans grew impatient with the slow moving and, to us, cumbersome methods of the foreigners.

When we left New York there were six or seven hundred trunks dumped into the hold of the *Ryndam*. Apparently, every trunk was at the bottom, and the limited porter service on the *Ryndam* made little headway in getting the baggage situation untangled. I lost all trace of my trunk between the Waldorf Astoria and the dock in New York. Of course I had a limited supply of clothing in my bags, but the uncertainty of its whereabouts finally drove me to make an effort to locate my trunk. This was after we left Los Angeles. But the more vigorously I talked to the cabin stewards, the more stolid they became. The Dutch are not an excitable race. In desperation, I finally got hold of a baggage man, and, stripped to the waist, I dragged him down to the baggage-room below the water level, where it was some degrees hotter than Hades, and we fell-to, lifting the trunks about in an effort to find mine. I was not the only one there either. A big, husky foot-ball star, who had flunked his exams the previous year, was likewise engaged with a perspiring Dutchman at his side, who hindered rather than helped. I heard the ex-star shout, "For the love of Mike, get out of the way and let me at that trunk! I am in a hurry." These and other similar expressions of American impatience at the average foreigner's more leisurely way of doing things,

FACULTY GROUP

Around the World at Seventeen

no doubt, have much to do with their love for us. As I have mentioned, it was extremely hot in the baggage-room. We could hear the roar and pounding of the ocean against the hull of the ship. There was little air in the hold and that little was laden with the pungent, acrid smell of sweating leather. I had never been sea-sick but now an inner voice, deep, deep down, whispered a warning. If I stayed in that inferno five minutes longer I realized what would happen, and I ate too frugally on shipboard to spare a single morsel. Fortunately, just then I found my long lost trunk and I got out of there in a hurry. Later, when I returned for it, I spent three hours in dragging, pushing, and carrying it from the baggage-hold to my quarters.

There were lots of minor odds and ends—fragments, I might say—that made up the six days from Los Angeles to Hilo, our first port of call in the Hawaiian Islands. One must remember that the captain's word is law on board ship. Naturally he must be a man of forceful character. Such was Captain Lieuwen. In addition to being master of the ship, he was a member of the faculty, being Dean of Navigation. He was a brusque man, not without a sense of humor—although in the following incident his humor was little appreciated. Going into the smoking-room, he approached a table where a group of

Around the World at Seventeen

students were playing poker, and looked on, smiling pleasantly.

"We are not playing for anything, Captain," said one of the boys, with a crafty eye on his pile of chips, which had a nice color effect, the blues predominating above the whites and reds. "Then," said the captain pleasantly, "these are not worth anything." And he reached over and jumbled the chips together into one pile.

There was a long silence among the dumbfounded players; and as the captain turned away he said, "No more gambling, boys."

Another time, the captain gave a few words of free advice to the uninitiated: "Those who ask fool questions about the position of the ship, of their room, or similar inanities, should write them to me and I will answer at my leisure. Another thing—if any one hits me on the back again, calling me 'steward,' and demanding to know, 'Where the hell is my room?' I'll punch him in the jaw!" As the captain weighed two hundred and was in fine condition, the hint sufficed.

When Vasco Núñez de Balboa gave the name of Pacific to the placid waters gently lapping the shores of Panama, he misnamed a considerable amount of territory, for the weather conditions of the above mentioned ocean were anything but pacific after we left San Pedro. Due to the heat, Worthington and I

Around the World at Seventeen

left our porthole open and one morning—October 14, to be exact—we were rudely awakened at five-thirty by a terrific *bang!* A wave had dashed through the porthole and had literally submerged us, drenching our bedding and clothes and slopping around on the floor a foot deep. For the first time we rose too early for breakfast.

From San Pedro to Hilo, the *Ryndam's* course described a great circle. Now every one knows, on a plane surface, the shortest distance between two points is a straight line, but on the surface of a sphere, the shortest distance between two points is the arc of a great circle passing through both points. The distance between the two above mentioned ports, by direct line W 240 S, is 2,145 miles, while the great circle distance is 2,133 miles, thus saving twelve miles, or one hour of travel, at the rate of the *Ryndam's* speed. To show further the influence of the earth's curvature on long voyages, take as an example the two ports San Francisco and Yokohama. A straight line between them measures 4,739 miles, while the great circle distance is 4,495 miles, a saving of 244 miles, or twenty hours, at the regular speed of the *Ryndam*.

The whole cruise looked forward to the Hawaiian Islands as being the first really important glimpse of a foreign country. Of course, politically speaking, it is one of Uncle Sam's possessions, and incidentally

Around the World at Seventeen

one of our largest military bases, with fifteen thousand troops stationed on the Island of Oahu. In order to inform myself about the Islands after leaving Los Angeles I devoted a good part of my time to reading books on Hawaii, in the extensive library of the ship.

On the morning of October 18, I looked expectantly through the porthole. In the hazy distance I saw what seemed first to be a white cloud-bank, low on the horizon. As the dawn advanced to day, the cloud-bank resolved itself into the snow-capped summit of Mauna Kea, the principal mountain of the Hawaiian Islands, with the famous volcano, Kilauea, rising to an elevation of 13,805 feet. Thirty miles nearer was the port of Hilo, as yet too low on the water's edge to be visible. Two hours later, at seven o'clock, we docked at the pier.

The attention showered upon strangers by the natives of the Hawaiian Islands lingers forever in the memory. No people in the world convey so delicately their simple, unaffected pleasure at having strangers among them. Scarcely had the boat touched the dock when eight native girls in white dresses, festooned in the flower wreath of the Islands, greeted the ship with cries of, "Welcome!" Behind them stood the crowd to which we had grown accustomed on entering every port. Yet, there was something different here; faces were alight with joy and antici-

Around the World at Seventeen

pation, rather than the curiosity which we had grown to expect.

While the girls sang, a native dancer did the hula-hula, which we applauded enthusiastically. By this time the gang-plank was lowered and we streamed ashore, every one of us having a *lei* tossed about our neck. The *lei* is a wreath of multi-colored flowers, bestowed upon all guests of the Islands. The fact that they are artificial detracts in nowise from their symbolism. The genuine *lei* sometimes is used but, comparatively, is expensive, requiring much time and labor to make.

The ceremony of welcome closed with the singers raising their voices in that most beautiful of all Hawaiian ballads, *Aloha Oe*—"Farewell to Thee." Then we made our way in a body to the automobiles that stood ready to convey us on various sight-seeing trips. Killick, Hart, Skinner, Robinson, and I were together, and we drew a Ford car, driven by a native named Fred, who spoke good English. I had already learned from experience that whether you saw little or much depended largely on securing the services of a good driver. In Fred we drew a jewel. Not only did he know the beaten trails but also the byways—to me always more interesting.

We were driven first through the streets of Hilo, which resembles a Kansas town of 10,000 inhabitants. Much of the population of Hilo consists of Japanese

Around the World at Seventeen

merchants and Chinese *poi* makers—*poi* being the *pièce de résistance* with all Hawaiian families. It is a food made from roots of the taro plant somewhat resembling our spinach. Hilo, second only to Honolulu in size and importance, is situated on a slope rising from the crescent-shaped bay. With its fine sand beach, it presents a beautiful sight from the sea. The main portion of the little city lies between two rivers. The principal residential quarter, Puueo, lies to the north of Wailuku River, while south of the Wailoa River is the Waiakea suburb, the headquarters of the fishing industry. After driving through Kamehameha Avenue, a broad, well-paved street, we continued on to the public school which is supported by the government.

We were informed that the school children had arranged a program and reception for the University Afloat. But we were totally unprepared for the experience in store for us. As our cars came to a halt before the well-lighted, spacious buildings, hundreds of native youngsters, drawn up in line on each side of the roadway, broke rank and crowded about us, literally burying us in flowers and trinkets. The great bouquets and woven clover *leis* were of blossoms of every color and scent. The trinkets consisted of little grass-woven mats, baskets, hand-worked doilies, and silk drawnwork handkerchiefs. They were not cheap gee-gaws such as one might expect as souvenirs

Around the World at Seventeen

on such occasion, but articles skillfully wrought, showing the patient labor of a thousand small hands. As your gift was presented, the little donor, with brown face beaming with gladness and pride, would say, "I give this to you because I made it with my own hands and I like the American students." The simplicity and sincerity moved one strangely. Here were hundreds of children of alien blood, belonging to a land which had lately come under the protection of the Stars and Stripes, paying their tribute to our common country in a demonstration to a body of visiting students from the homeland.

Following the gift-giving the children sang their national ballads and some songs in English. When they struck up *America* their voices vibrated with patriotic fervor and every member of the cruise sprang to his feet and stood at attention. We American born, who are accustomed to the privileges and benefits of a free, democratic country, never pause in our mad rush to show appreciation of this great land of ours. It takes the foreign-born, who come from a country less prodigal with its gifts, to be ever grateful to their adopted land. I have, on many occasions, stood in great concourses of people suddenly aroused to patriotic fervor. I have thrilled at those demonstrations. But the spontaneous outburst of patriotism of these Hawaiian children singing my national anthem stirred me more than I can tell.

Around the World at Seventeen

We later learned that the school was given a vacation to prepare for our reception, and weeks before-hand the children had worked industriously with their little brown hands to make presents with which to assure us of our welcome. After we bade them farewell, we departed for a drive to the volcano of Kilauea, followed by the sweetly-sad strains of *Aloha Oe*.

CHAPTER FIVE

I HAD just witnessed the demonstration of a peaceful and happy people. I wish I could as easily tell about the trip from sea-level to Kilauea that carried us to an elevation of over 13,000 feet. Thus far, Hilo had been an agreeable surprise, but when I look back on the thirty-mile drive to the volcano, at the contrasts and the multitude of natural phenomenon, I am at a loss to know where to begin.

One's first glimpse of the Islands on entering the crescent-shaped bay of Hilo is deceptive. The vegetation inland is so dense and uniform that from a distance it resembles a rising grassy plateau. In reality, it is an unbroken jungle—save for the plantation clearings—almost all the way to Kilauea. Climate rather than rich soil accounts for the luxuriant growth. In the lagoons, graceful palms, like long-handled, green-feather dusters, rimmed the placid waters. Grotesque shapes come to view unexpectedly, as if Nature in a freakish moment would dumbfound the beholder. This comes of the Islands being of volcanic origin. The wayfarer will come suddenly upon a native, with his little cottage hidden in an over-growth of ferns and flowers, perched on a shelf

Around the World at Seventeen

of rock in some out-of-the-way nook, where the waters give him sea-food and the land produces varieties of papaya, mangoes, breadfruit, cocoanuts, pineapples, bananas and guavas.

In all climes, primitive man based his legends upon his conflicts with nature. Due to the volcanic origin of the Hawaiian Islands, the legends of the natives teem with gods and demi-gods who hurled fiery bowlders at the hapless natives or made the earth tremble under their mighty footsteps. One wonders at what epoch of their progress the Islanders emerged from fear-ridden creatures into the present smiling, happy race.

Across the channel from Hilo lies Molokai, Cocoanut Island. The legend goes that when the demi-god, Maui, with his magic hook fished the Island up from the sea, one of his brothers in the canoe with him disregarded the demi-god's command not to look back. The charm being thus broken, the Island slipped back to its present location, and only a small portion remained above the sea. To-day, this legend remnant is Hilo's famous bathing resort.

Fred, our Hawaiian driver, proved to be a good sport. As he drove along, he taught us a few phrases in the Hawaiian language. We felt we needed appropriate expressions to use in case we met the native belles. One of these expressions I still remember—"One ka ouiki-ouiki"—"Kiss me again." At every

Around the World at Seventeen

girl we passed, we shouted this salutation—or would you say request? They blushed and giggled and sometimes made answer. But Fred would never tell us what they said, although their rejoinders aroused him to storms of mirth.

There is no road anywhere better than the one leading to the summit of Mauna Kea. But for the difference in vegetation and physical features of the landscape, I might imagine I was on one of the numerous famous driveways in the States. After leaving the confines of Hilo and the outlying scattered settlements, we plunged into a tropical jungle of huge, drooping, wet ferns, twenty feet and more high, which crowded the roadway on each side.

The monotony of the view, however, was broken at short intervals by sugar cane plantations. Sugar raising is the main industry of the Islands and the plantations and mills are among the largest in the world. Indeed, it is said the science of cultivating and milling sugar cane here attains a higher degree of perfection than in any other country. Running water is abundant in the Islands, and one of its uses is to convey the sugar cane in great flumes from plantation to mill.

In a view obtained of Rainbow Falls, I was surprised to see in the distance a structure that for the moment transported me to the border of the Rio Grande where the High Bridge on the Southern Pa-

Around the World at Seventeen

cific Railroad crosses the Pecos River. That bridge, perhaps, you know, is over three hundred feet high. The structure I now beheld resembled it, with its white lattice-work of girders and pillars supporting a great flume where it crosses the deep canyon above Rainbow Falls.

Sugar cane requires an abundance of water. One plantation alone uses as much as the city of San Francisco. It has been estimated that it requires half a ton of water to produce a pound of sugar. There are forty-seven sugar-producing corporations on the Islands, and Hawaii's output is exceeded only by Cuba and Java.

Besides numerous sugar plantations, we encountered great pineapple groves, "checker-boarded" like Kansas corn fields, resembling battalions of porcupines in marching formation. The pineapple output of the Islands is one half as great as all the canned-fruit output of California.

There is a legend about Rainbow Falls that also deals with the demi-god, Maui. The goddess, Hina, lived in a great cave under the falls. A dragon, Kuna-Moo, tried to drown her by throwing up a dam, thus backing the water into her retreat. Hina called for aid to her son, Maui, who was at the time in Haleakala, trying to lasso the sun. He crossed the ocean in his canoe in two strides and chased the dragon to the Boiling Pots, some distance below the falls, where

Around the World at Seventeen

he threw red-hot stones into the water, scalding the monster, which he finally killed. It is worth noting that all the legends of the Islands are built around the history of volcanic activities.

What had seemed from the ship a broad grassy plateau now proved to be a rugged, broken country with great sugarloaf mountains and precipitous crevices where one finds Iao Valley, the "Yosemite of Hawaii." The ascent was gradual; at no time did we strike steep grades, but the change in respiration indicated the higher altitude, and finally we came to a halt a brief walk from the famous crater.

I must confess that Kilauea was a disappointment. All the pictures I had seen showed the crater a great smoking sea of red-hot lava, with flames reaching heavenward like a burning oil-well. What I really saw was a huge basin, eight miles in circumference, said to be large enough to hold Manhattan Island, rimmed with large rocky crevices from which smoke poured in jets. Kilauea, unlike the natives, had planned no reception for us; it lay as if asleep, breathing heavy black steam. But as I write, word comes that after a long quiet, the dreaded volcano has again roused to activity.

The majority of the members of the cruise visited Volcano House, the commodious hotel and resting place directly overlooking the crater. My gang, however, craved more excitement. Besides, we were hun-

Around the World at Seventeen

gry. We held a consultation with Fred, our driver, who volunteered to show us some sights not included in the regular itinerary. With our trusty Ford "hitting on all four" we nosed the wind back toward Hilo.

When we expressed our desire for food, the best and lots of it, Fred smiled knowingly and said, "Leave it to me!" And we knew we were in the hands of a good Samaritan. But in order to whet our appetites to an even keener edge, our driver detoured from the Hilo road, into the Fern Jungle, the most famous of its kind in the world. To reach the jungle we got out of the car and by means of steps climbed through the the lava tube, a great tunnel two hundred yards long, with a floor of hardened lava as slick as glass. By the aid of search-lights, we found our way through this phenomenon to the Fern Jungle at the other end of the lava flow. Here were ferns of every description, among them the bird's-nest and fish-tail *ekaha*, almost as large as trees. The Hawaiians weave the long, graceful fronds of the ferns, or ekaha, about their hats, and every home in Hawaii, no matter how humble, is beautified by this decorative plant. So dense overhead were the interlaced fronds that no air or sunlight penetrated. A dozen native Boy Scouts met us and conducted us around the shady paths, cool with moisture that dripped from the leaves overhead. Nor could we see the tips of the ferns, so dense was the foliage.

Around the World at Seventeen

It was already two p. m., and we had breakfasted early. But when a native sets out to play host he generally knows what he is about. Once again in the car we drove to the outskirts of Hilo, where Fred conducted us to a famous winery. There we saw acres of grape vines laden with grapes of all colors—white, lavender and blue. We were shown the huge vats where the wine is made. The winery is noted for its Jamaica rum also, very old and fine.

All we now needed was chop suey to complete our happiness; and Fred was able to spot the best in Hilo. We soon found ourselves in an upstairs Chinese restaurant, in a private room overlooking the street, where we settled comfortably in anticipation of the forthcoming feast. Fred spoke a few cabalistic words in Chinese to the boss who glanced at us, kotowing and grinning. When he shuffled away we resigned ourselves for the usual long wait. Suddenly, somewhere a jazz band struck up the tune "Yes, Sir, That's My Baby!" We stared at each other in amazement; then everybody rushed to the windows. Up the street came a big automobile-bus, with great streamers along the running board telling the world of Hilo that the "Original California Minstrel Show" was in town. A big negro in a shining silk top-hat and long black frock coat was leading the show.

I yelled down to him, "Hello, Sam! Are you from California?"

Around the World at Seventeen

He glanced up, his face shining with joy on beholding a fellow countryman, and he said, "Lawdy, boss, I'ze sho' glad to see yo'! No, sah, we's from Alabam'!"

He was glad to see us and he stopped the car and struck up the music. Shortly, the chop suey was brought in and you can imagine how five hungry American lads spent the next hour, keeping time with the jazz band below. After the meal, we bade Fred farewell, making his heart glad with a liberal tip, and went on board the boat which was to sail at five o'clock. We pulled off with the crowd shouting, "Come back!" while hundreds of voices were raised in singing *Aloha Oe*. We called it a day and turned in for the night run to Honolulu.

Hilo, which we had just left, is second only to Honolulu, in size and importance. It is situated on the Island of Hawaii. Hilo takes its name from the crescent-shaped harbor, the word meaning new moon. The harbor is called Byron Bay, after a cousin of the poet, who arrived in 1824 in command of the British frigate, *Blende*, landing there with the bodies of King Kamehameha II and his queen, both of whom had succumbed to measles in London.

As before suggested, the Islands of Hawaii are made of the lava flow from five volcanoes, three of which can be seen from Hilo. Towering in the background is Mauna Kea, the highest mountain in the Pacific, 13,823 feet. Not so high by a scant two hundred

Around the World at Seventeen

feet, but reputed to be the largest volcano in the world, stands Mauna Loa, and Kilauea.

Of course, one can not help being struck forcibly by the dearth of wild animals in a land where jungle solitude assures protection. This is accounted for by the two thousand miles of ocean that lie between the Islands and the nearest mainland. The day-flying bat is the only warm-blooded mammal. Lizards, land-snails, owls, buzzards and the curious little song-birds, called honey-suckers, abound. Man's contribution includes mosquitoes and cockroaches. It is not certain just when the latter contributions were made, but it is fair to assume it was with the coming of the first white man, Don Juan Gastona, a Spaniard, about 1555. When Captain James Cook landed on the Islands, in 1778, he found traces of the earlier Spanish expedition in numerous fair-skinned, red-haired natives.

The Islands are the only stepping-stone between the American continent and Asia. At various times England and France made unsuccessful attempts to bring them under control. Finally, for military reasons, they were voluntarily annexed to the United States, in 1898.

It was hot on shipboard, but despite the discomfort, I slept soundly until 6:30 the next morning when I was awakened by shouts outside my porthole. I arose, dressed, and went on deck to learn the cause of the commotion.

CHAPTER SIX

WE were still five miles out from the port of Honolulu. Under the lee of our vessel, two outrigger canoes, paddled vigorously by natives, glided smoothly along on the glassy sea. Like bees swarming about their hives, scores of Kanakas swam with one hand, while with the other held aloft they shouted greetings to the vessel. They had swum out five miles to meet us, using the two canoes for the purpose of an occasional rest. Their cries awoke the ship, and as quickly as we could dress, we crowded to the rails to watch them. With the instinct of the ballyhoo who shouts to attract his crowd at the side-show, the natives now began to "sell" their idea. There rose the cries of "Nickely! Dimey!" and we responded with a shower of coins that spattered the calm, placid waters like raindrops.

The scene reminded one of a school of porpoises at play. These divers were the most graceful specimens of manhood I had ever seen. Hawaiians love the water; they live in it so much they have almost become amphibians. They perform incredible feats. The moment a coin left your hand, a diver followed the arc of its course with his eyes, while he darted to the spot where it would fall on the waters. Some-

Around the World at Seventeen

times, he caught the coin in the air; at others, he recovered it as it disappeared beneath the surface and he came up grinning, thrusting the coin between his shining, white teeth. At first, I dropped my coins too near the boat side to get my money's worth of fun. The diver I chose recovered them too easily. So I played with him, making false motions, finally throwing the coin high and far. Invariably he was at the spot when the coin struck the water.

In this wise, we steamed into the harbor of Honolulu, the swimmers playing around the boat like so many glistening, brown-bodied porpoises. The most thrilling moment of all came when the *Ryndam* nosed up to the dock, with only a few feet of space between hull and wall. Several of the more daring divers continued what had become a dangerous sport. The space between hull and dock narrowed to ten feet, eight feet, six feet, before the last of the divers darted out of danger, with a final wave of his hand and with nickels, dimes and quarters bulging his cheeks. It was estimated the divers recovered between two and three hundred dollars—not a poor morning's work for lads ranging in age from fifteen to twenty-two.

Our attention turned from the divers to the reception awaiting us. The ship had drawn up to a great double-decked, white dock where, to the strains of a wonderful band playing *Aloha Oe*, a crowd of four

Around the World at Seventeen

hundred people, mostly Americans, bade us welcome. We disembarked and sought the usual fleet of automobiles. Our gang—Killick, Skinner, Robinson, and myself—prompted by a flare up of *E Pluribus Unum*, that is, democratic fervor, not unshrewdly choosing our driver rather than the sumptuousness of our car, spied an old Buick, which held our fascinated eyes. It was of the vintage of 1912, in color a battered, washed-out red, by far the shabbiest of the lot—a modern one-horse shay—only the word modern is not appropriate. But the driver was all we could desire, in appearance, in speech, in knowledge—Jim Davis, by name, with cauliflower ears and a Bowery accent, and knowing Honolulu as a beauty knows her rouge-box. He immediately proved our faith in him by maneuvering his old bus to the second position in the line of the hundred cars. Wheezing and puffing and knocking together its worn metal joints, it meandered down the street behind the lead car, a magnificent Rolls Royce limousine. The latter was a deep green—with envy, no doubt, at the greater attention and smiles showered upon our modest shay.

The drive through the business section of Honolulu reminded me forcibly that we had not yet left America. The buildings were modern, and the pedestrians appeared to be going somewhere in a great hurry. The weather was perfect. We turned from the downtown section along a broad, paved boulevard that led

Around the World at Seventeen

up a gradually rising hill to the English and American winter homes, which are surrounded by tropical flowers and plants of vivid hues—bright red, green, yellow, lavender—embracing almost every flower and shrub known to temperate climes.

This broad highway led us in time to the topmost rise, terminating at the Pali—the Cliffs—where suddenly we apparently came to the end of the world. Getting out of our car, we walked to the edge and looked down two thousand feet into a wonderful valley checker-boarded with tiny plantations. One felt as a god beholding the earth from the heavens. The remoteness, the silence, reaching up at us from the valley below, were truly inspiring. That view from the Pali, is, beyond doubt, the most magnificent Hawaii has to offer the traveler. The road at the edge of the great cliffs broadens into an amphitheater, with hills on all sides save that of the precipice. Beyond the fertile valley stretches the ocean, lost in the dim distance of the horizon.

A fascinating story is told about Kamehameha, the first king of the Hawaiian Islands. He was born on a wild night with the prophecy attached to his name that he would conquer the rival kings and establish a single dynasty. In accordance with this prophecy, he fought a great battle on the slope leading to the Pali, slowly forcing the enemy ever nearer the cliffs. At the crucial moment, with every avenue of escape

Around the World at Seventeen

cut off by his warriors, he directed a final offensive with the main body of his army and forced the foe over the precipice. It is said twenty thousand of his enemies were destroyed.

On the return trip from the Pali, an amusing incident occurred. Our ancient shay emitted a series of metallic groans, gave a final gasp, and went dead. Fortunately it was on a down grade, and we maneuvered the old bus around and headed for town. With the engine silent we drifted grandly along, trailing the Rolls Royce limousine, with Jim Davis, proudly erect, directing our course. At the first service station we dropped out of line—it gave us a good excuse to shake the excursion anyhow.

As we drew up to the station, the proprietor came forward to learn our needs, and, with great dignity, Jim enumerated the casualities and requested they be immediately fixed. Just then a tire blew out with a loud *bang!* Jim looked around dazedly, but without change of voice or manner he included the new casualty in the list. The mishap, however, was not a total loss, for during the rejuvenating process, we found seats at a table on the balcony of a tea house surrounded by a beautiful garden and, with a cool ocean breeze lulling us, we sipped various refreshing drinks.

Provided our shay still held together, we intended next to visit the beach of Waikiki. After a time we

Around the World at Seventeen

were able to continue our journey and with the exception of two more blow-outs we safely reached the famous Moana Hotel. This hotel is the last word in luxury. It is a white, six-story structure, built on three sides of a quadrangle, facing the beach promenade of Waikiki. It is very old and rich in traditions. We left the car and strolled out under the tall, graceful palms, for our first view of the famous beach. In the background, nestled a number of neat cottages, which we were told can be rented at reasonable rates. We decided that when we again visited the Islands, it would be a good idea to rent one.

On first entering the harbor, we had a splendid view of Diamond Head, a massive, jutting diamond-shaped pile of rock which stands in the same relation to the Hawaiian Islands as Gibraltar does to the Mediterranean Sea. Here a fortress garrisoned by our troops controls the coast for many miles. Later when I saw Gibraltar, I thought it much less impressive after this second view of Diamond Head from Waikiki beach.

There are a number of distinctive features about Waikiki beach. One can walk a mile from the shore, with the water of uniform depth—not over one's head. Those who can swim, however, are warned against "traps," scooped-out holes of great depth, which occasionally occur. Killick and I later had an experience in one of these "traps" that almost cost

Around the World at Seventeen

us our lives. I will reserve that account for the last, where indeed it belongs, for it ended our swim.

White swimmers, only, are allowed on the beach. The life-guards, however, who are natives, are fine-looking fellows. Killick and I watched a number of bathers with outrigger canoes and surf-boards, and decided to try our hands at the sport. We donned bathing suits and very foolishly started wading out from the shore as we do at our home beaches. It was then I met a disappointment; the floor of the beach is composed of sharp, glass-edged coral and before I could halt, the soles of my feet were painfully lacerated. Then I thought I knew why surf-boards and boats were used.

The thrill of my surf-boat ride will linger with me as long as I am capable of thrills. Your native canoe-man paddles straight for the open ocean. The beach is a mile away, seen only when the canoe rides the crest of the leaping waves. Into the trough of the sea you drop, and out again. The canoe-man swings his craft shoreward. He bides his time. A mountainous wave is dashing toward you with the speed of an express train. Frantically, the oarsman begins to paddle. The outrigger canoe, resembling a huge, brown tarantula carrying a bamboo pole on each side, gains speed—and darts nose-first into the trough, with the huge waves pressing hard upon the stern of the paper-shell craft. Suddenly you are lifted, literally

Around the World at Seventeen

thrown, out of the trough onto the crest of the whitecapped mountain which has overtaken you. You are in the grip of that shoreward drive, and now standing motionless, the native steers his course, your canoe shooting forward, up and down on the frothy crest at a speed of thirty or forty miles an hour. Exciting, yes! An aeroplane, nose-diving, banking, and turning somersaults in the air offers nothing more thrilling. The smoothness of our flight without bumps or jars, without fear of blow-outs, too, excels the racing automobile for sport. Not until within a few feet of the shore does the canoe lessen speed; and then you do it again and again, until you are sated with the thrill of it. Thus, one learns why outrigger canoes are so popular.

I next tried my hand with a surf-board with not nearly so much success, because I had to do my own inexpert paddling. The surf-boards are probably as old as the earliest inhabitants and a ceremony is connected with its making. Surf-riding is identified in a remote way with the ceremonies and superstitions of kakuuaism—witchery. In earlier times, gambling was carried on in connection with the sport, lending a fascination to the game which caused the natives to spend many hours on the water that should have been spent in their fields. Three kinds of trees are used in making the surf-boards—the *wiliwili, ulu* or bread fruit, and the *loa*. The red *kumu* fish is placed at the

Around the World at Seventeen

foot of the tree selected to be cut down, a hole is dug at its roots and the fish is buried with a prayer in payment thereof. The trunk is chipped away on two opposite sides until it is reduced to a board. When the surface has been smoothed by the means of coral instruments, the plank is stained with a root die until it attains a glossy, black surface.

I tried for two hours before I mastered the knack of the thing. After every unsuccessful attempt I had to paddle out to the starting point. It was no mean stunt to lie face downward, with your arms hanging over the sides like oars. It was more exertion than pulling the old sled back up the hill. But when I did connect with the waves my board swept shoreward, with me standing erect and my hands behind my head—an exhilarating and strenuous exercise.

Finding the water so pleasant, Killick and I, for the moment forgetting the "traps" against which we were warned, decided to swim out a mile or so from shore. There could be no danger where at any moment we could touch bottom and rest. Consequently, we swam until our strength was almost spent and the Moana Hotel was a speck in the distance. We were alone and weary but having a good time. The good time ceased, however, when we attempted to touch bottom. Killick was nearly played out and I was not much better off. When we failed to find bottom, we decided we had struck a "trap," and we

Around the World at Seventeen

swam desperately for a hundred yards to pass over it. Again we failed to touch bottom. The situation was becoming desperate. Killick complained of a cramp, and I had no reserve strength to offer him. I shouted encouragement and turned on my back to float and rest. Killick did likewise. In this manner after an interminable time we crawled out on the coral beach some distance from the Moana hotel, so exhausted that we lay panting and weak for two hours before we could make our way back to Waikiki beach. Why we failed to touch bottom remains a mystery to this good day. The only satisfying conclusion we could reach was that we swam out over a ship channel and unconsciously followed it back to shore.

Killick and I dressed and went to the Moana Hotel, where we lunched and mailed post-cards home. Then we had Jim Davis drive us to the Alexander Young Hotel, in Honolulu, where we registered for ourselves and Skinner, the latter joining us in time to dine.

In the evening, we again called on Jim Davis and his trusty shay to show us the "bright lights" of Honolulu. This he did to our complete satisfaction. On the round, we took a look-see into Jew Sam's where the principal drink served is the native *okolehau*, a pale, watery-looking beverage of deceptive strength and belated "kick."

The next day was the last in Honolulu and I further practiced with the surf-board and scouted in the downtown section in search of food for later consumption on shipboard. I also sent a radiogram home and went out to Diamond Head for a closer view of the fortified bluff. While on that trip I paid a visit to the aquarium which is quite famous for the variety and color of its fish.

We had a memorable lunch at the Moana Hotel and last of all before boarding the *Ryndam*, the finest chop suey I ever tasted, in a cobwebby Chinese joint, hidden away under the eaves of a dilapidated native house. The rats and mice, playing around us on the floor, failed to lessen our appreciation of the occasion.

I departed the shores of Hawaii with real regret. Really, to see the Islands one should have at least a month in which to poke leisurely around in the out-of-way places. There were other beaches much better than Waikiki and even more romantic—for instance that of Kailua. Like all tropical countries the spell of romance is strongest in the moonlight. But to enjoy moonlight nights one must have leisure, and I could only rush madly from place to place in order to see even a little. The most impressive thing about the Islands, I should say, is the natives' patriotic love of country, and their kindness and good manners, all of which contribute toward making them the wonderful hosts they are.

At five p.m., October 21, the *Ryndam* quitted the dock for the thirteen day trip to Yokohama, putting

Around the World at Seventeen

before us the prospect of another tiresome ocean voyage. Our departure was a sad affair. My sentiments were shared by almost every one on board, and were heightened by the sad strains of the band and the farewell shouts of the crowd at the dock.

There is a quaint and touching ceremony in connection with a ship's departure from the Islands. From the wealth of wreaths of flowers showered by the natives upon the traveler, one is saved, which he casts upon the waters after the vessel reaches the open ocean. If his wreath is carried back to the shore by the waves, he will again visit Hawaii. I certainly hope mine landed safely.

CHAPTER SEVEN

THE most of us were glad enough to have a few days rest after our strenuous three days in Hawaii. We took up our studies where we had left off six days before and the ship settled down to the usual monotony of an ocean voyage. I was somewhat consoled, however, by the thought that after leaving Yokohama there would be no more long sea trips; that the greater part of our time would be spent seeing new and strange sights and coming in contact with interesting peoples.

In looking back, there are a number of things worth noting on this our longest unbroken sea trip. For one thing, we crossed the International "Date Line," which was established in 1839, whereby one day of the week is lost or gained. When, on the Line, it was 11:59 p.m., October 26; October 25 was just ending on the eastern side of the Line. A minute later it is October 27,—hence the vessel going west skips from October 25 to October 27. Vessels going west skip a day; those going east enjoy two of the same date.

As October 26 was our "Lost Day," our week foreshortened to six days. As I had Physical Education on Monday, Wednesday, and Friday, it was necessary for me to attend the class two days in succession. If

Around the World at Seventeen

we had been sailing eastward, our week would have had eight days, and I suppose I would have had double classes on the two Tuesdays. After all, I was glad we were sailing westward.

Despite the fact that we struck the Japanese current, with the vessel progressing steadily northward, the weather grew hotter each day. Two days off the coast of Japan I caught my first glimpse of the Orient. The sea was calm and a deep green. A half dozen Japanese fishing junks with their odd, bat-wing-shaped sails hanging motionless, had little, brown, half-naked Japs on deck waving at us.

Five days out from Japan a curious thing happened. A golden plover, differing slightly from the American bird of that species, lit on the rigging of the *Ryndam* and was captured by Mrs. Frazier, who gave it the appropriate name, *Quo Vadis*. The bird was exhausted after its long flight, presumably from the Hawaiian or South Sea Islands. The spot at which he made his landing was perhaps the point farthest from land in any ocean of the world. At first *Quo Vadis* could only peck at cracker crumbs and nozzle the water given him. But he was placed in a cage, where he seemed quite content and thrived on puffed rice, corn flakes, and lettuce. However, he did not touch meat or fish, proving he was not a habitual seafarer. A storm probably blew him out to sea and fortunately he found a haven on the *Ryndam*

Around the World at Seventeen

before he was exhausted. We all considered *Quo Vadis* an omen of good luck.

Two days out from Yokohama, Captain Lieuwen ordered the speed of the boat cut down as we were running ahead of schedule. Impatient as we were to reach the port this news spread consternation over the ship. As a matter of fact, we slipped into the harbor so quietly that we were unaware of our arrival at Yokohama until one of the fellows thrust his head into the door of the smoking-room, where a group of us were playing bridge, and shouted, "Japan!" This was at one o'clock November 4, the day before we were supposed to arrive.

Although I had heard Japan called "The Land of the Setting Sun," I did not know how literally true this was until I rushed on deck and found the world enveloped in a murky fog that one could cut with a knife. Setting sun was right! We could feel the little tugs shunting us about; could hear their engines throb, while on all sides rose a medley of sounds from the deep-throated fog-horns. When we reached the long white dock, the fog was not so dense and objects became visible to our eager eyes. Already we anticipated going ashore.

But first we must pass through the usual customs and health inspection. This is an ordeal, if the captain of the vessel is unobliging or crusty. Captain Lieuwen, however, was a wise old salt. When the

Around the World at Seventeen

Japanese customs officers and doctors came on board they found every man Jack, and every lady "Jackette," standing in a double line that completely circled the promenade deck. The Japanese returned courtesy for courtesy. What might have proved a disagreeable experience became merely a matter of every one's answering to his name as it was called by the officials. Our passports were turned over to the authorities who retired to the smoking-room to examine them.

It was now five o'clock and we looked forward to seeing Yokohama by night. Imagine our dismay when we were told shore-leave began at eight o'clock the next morning. The majority of us resigned ourselves to the all night wait, and spent the time discussing Japan and planning various private expeditions. But sleep was out of the question. At all hours we could hear boys climbing down the side of the vessel on ropes, bent on seeing Yokohama by night. Sixty-five managed to "escape." I was rather glad I did not go myself as the report was brought back that the city was literally buried in mud, with jinrickshas stuck in the streets.

The next morning, Killick, Robinson, and I were among the first off the boat. We passed through a massive, well-arranged dock building, and emerged upon the sidewalk facing a street of one and two story buildings placarded with signs in huge Japa-

Around the World at Seventeen

nese characters. My first impression was that I beheld a Mah Jong set. I can come no nearer describing the scene. Japan is so different, even the landscapes, the trees and flowers. The buildings are so grotesque and foreign to our idea of architecture; the manners and customs are so strange that one is at a loss to establish a standard of comparison. Nor can I hope to express adequately the thousands of interesting sights and experiences among which I lived during my six days in the Flowery Kingdom. I can only make the feeble effort without further apology.

Our plans were vague. A. M. Mizzlewitz, a former Kansas City newspaper man, was an editor on the *Japan Advertiser,* the largest American paper in Japan. Paul Robinson had known him at the University of Missouri, and received a note from "Mizzie" asking us to meet him at the Imperial Hotel, Tokyo. Therefore, we were Tokyo bound.

Beyond the one fact, our ideas were limited to zero. We were without passports—the officials still had them; in a strange country, among people who jealously guard their peculiar customs and who probably would resent any slight unconsciously placed upon them. We felt the moment we set foot in Yokohama that here our ignorance would not serve as an excuse. Of course, it was optional with us to remain with the cruise and be "close-herded"—to use a Western expression—along paths of safety. Such, however, was

Around the World at Seventeen

not our intention, and we looked forward to the adventures that surely were in store for us.

Tokyo bound! What move to make to get there called for weighty consideration. In the first place, it was foggy and bitter cold—the weather here we found was similar to that of Kansas City in November; but we had donned heavy clothing and overcoats for the occasion. Coolies were everywhere, warming themselves around little fires. Women in kimonos and wearing funny wooden shoes—cloth sandals are worn only in dry weather—mingled with the men. Some of them carried children on their backs swathed in shawls or in little baskets. Jinrickshas, high, rubber-tired, wire-wheeled carts, stood waiting for fares, with typical Japanese lanterns, burning brightly, suspended from their backs.

We bargained with three ricksha men to take us to the railroad station. We felt like the Three Musketeers, perched high in the air where we could look down upon the tiny but sturdy Nipponese swarming about us. The proverbial lack of privacy of the gold fish was privacy indeed compared to ours. We jogged off down a gravel street, three abreast, very erect and stiff, with our new kind of cabbies uniformly dressed in short-belted black smocks, straw umbrella hats, tight trousers, and odd-looking rubber shoes. These shoes, by the way, fitted the feet like gloves and never came off. The ricksha coolie has thin arms but huge

Around the World at Seventeen

legs and calves, and as he jogs along his over-developed muscles gather in knots with every stride.

We eventually came to a river, I should say one hundred feet wide, spanned by a high bridge. In crossing, we beheld another scene typically Japanese. As far as the eye could penetrate the fog, the river bristled with the masts of fishing boats—a sampan fleet just arousing to the new day. On the prows of these queer-looking crafts, great eyes were painted supposedly to enable the fishermen to see the fish; on others horns were carved to frighten the fish. Tiny lanterns hung everywhere on the sampans and the fishermen's families huddled about little fires, cooking their breakfasts of rice. These fishing junks were so thick that one could easily cross the river by stepping from one to the other.

On all sides, we beheld signs of the disastrous earthquake in Yokohama in 1923. Translated, Yokohama means "sea-side beach." Situated on Tokyo Bay, it is the principal sea port of Japan. One notes with amazement and considerable respect the courage and industry of the little Jap and the immense strides which have been made in rebuilding during the last three years. Japanese shops are usually one story affairs—although more pretentious and modern buildings everywhere are under construction. The building material of these shops consists largely of *papier-mâché* and a sort of composition made from sea shells.

Around the World at Seventeen

This composition is transparent and gives light to the interior of the buildings, the windows merely being apertures to admit air, usually sliding open and shut. Other houses were constructed of cheap wood and rice straw matting. Matting likewise generally serves for the floor covering. Vacant lots were everywhere, and the remains of the buildings destroyed by fire during the great quake, were mute evidence of that stupendous calamity.

Very noticeable to the traveler is the over-population of Japan. Streets of ordinary consequence were teeming with people in a manner one expects to find only on Broadway and State Streets.

Perhaps it was this sense of over-crowding that gave us the gold-fishy sensation. On all sides, I imagined the Japanese casting sinister glances at us. I endeavored to whistle up my courage and leaned backward in the ricksha. Instantly my coolie looked around, chattering something which I took to be Japanese oaths. Just what custom I had violated did not strike me instantly but my man made signs for me to lean forward. Then I understood. If the passenger in a ricksha leans back far enough he can literally lift his cabby off the ground. Down the street we went leaning forward as if we had eaten something that failed to agree with us. In this bent position, we finally gained the covered railroad station.

Around the World at Seventeen

Our next encounter was with Japanese money. Before leaving the *Ryndam* I had bought in exchange what I thought to be enough yens and sens to see me through. It takes two yen to make a dollar and one hundred sen equals one yen; therefore, it takes two sen to make a cent of our money. We had heard the ricksha men were highbinders and robbers; the reader can draw his own conclusion whether the assertion is true. After considerable argument, in which no one understood what the other fellow said, we compromised by paying in full a total of three yen—fifty cents to each of the three for the privilege of dragging us several miles through muddy streets!

We looked in vain for the railroad station and finally found a ticket window where a woman smiled out at us. The Japanese smile on most all occasions; even to the great god Buddha whose grin has never lessened through the centuries. Whatever the occasion, the smile is there. They laugh at the least excuse—and sometimes without any. A Japanese imparting the sad intelligence of his Mother's death will probably say, "Mother died last night, ha! ha!"

After purchasing our tickets to Tokyo, from the smiling, kimonoed lady, we found our way up a stair to an elevated railroad. We checked our baggage, or rather had it stamped, at a cost of four sen, or two cents, per piece. While waiting for the train we observed our surroundings. Along each side of the

Around the World at Seventeen

tracks and platforms stretched gardens of beautiful flowers. There also was a news and cigar stand. Except for the flower bed, the station reminded me of the Chicago "L."

Japan is full of surprises, but none greater than the railway service. Between Yokohama and Tokyo, a distance of nineteen miles, electric trains, operated by the third rail system, leave the Sakuragicho station every twelve minutes. Judging from the crowd about us, this excellent service is well patronized by the home folk.

On entering our compartment, we found an American, the first we had seen since leaving the boat. He sat by a window reading the *Japan Advertiser*. No, he was not Mizzlewitz, but A. Bland Calder, the American Commercial Attaché, who fell to chuckling on hearing us discuss with considerable animation our impressions of Japan. Learning we were bound for Tokyo, he introduced himself and invited us to accompany him to the Truscon Steel Plant, at Shimbashi, two stations from Tokyo. Later, he would escort us to the Imperial Hotel. Mr. Calder proved a useful friend. He knew the country and the language. When we left the train to take a motor bus to the steel plant, the driver of a rickety, old carryall, seeing foreign prey, tried to engage himself for the trip at double price. His astonishment was equaled only by his chagrin when Mr. Calder addressed him

Around the World at Seventeen

in fluent Japanese. We could only judge what the attaché said by the expression of the driver's face, but evidently it sufficed for the man drove rapidly away.

We finally got into a Ford bus and went at breakneck speed through streets barely wide enough for our car. After a breath-taking interval of this, we arrived at the steel plant. It was a huge affair. The entire office force, superintendent and foremen, was composed of Englishmen, who greeted us pleasantly and took pains to show us the inner workings of the plant. Coolie labor was used, manning the hoists and crane carriages, stoking holes, and puddling machinery. On looking back over the visit, one thing stands out more clearly than any other—we Americans push a saw from us, the coolies pull it toward them. As all industrial plants in Japan are the last word in moderism, equal in efficiency and output to any of our own, and as I am no steel expert, I will not attempt to give a detailed description of this great plant, although the different stages the raw material passes through to emerge as the finest grade of steel in the Flowery Kingdom were explained fully to us.

We returned to the station by the same bus which brought us and boarded the first train for Tokyo. Railroad travel in Japan brings home clearly the overpopulation of the country, a subject on which I have already touched. Of the 149,000 square miles comprising the total area of Japan proper, according to

Around the World at Seventeen

the report of the Department of Agriculture and Forestry, only 15 per cent is tillable. The remaining 85 per cent consists of cities, towns, and village area, mountains, lakes, rivers, forests, and waste lands. Between Yokohama and Tokyo, you no sooner leave a town than you enter another. For this reason, I judge, the railroads are elevated. The speed at which the trains travel would be out of the question if they had to slow down for the street crossings as they do in our country. The railroads and most of the hotels are owned and operated by the Imperial Government.

CHAPTER EIGHT

LEAVING the train at the Tokyo station, we descended from the elevated into the most imposing structure in size I was ever in, not excepting the Pennsylvania Railroad Station in New York. It is one of the great railroad terminals of the world and, strange to say, was unharmed by fire or earthquake in 1923. We passed out of the main entrance into a plaza and there the magnitude of the station struck us. It covers two long city blocks, is three to five stories high, and has two enormous domes which balance each other near the ends. It was of Western architectural design, as were the large office buildings across the plaza in which we now stood. Among the latter was a prominent eight story building, the largest structure of its kind east of Suez.

My impression of Tokyo was that of one entering any modern American city, although later I found the introduction of Western architecture, ways, and ideas, had not produced many changes in the lives and customs of the majority of the people in Japan.

Before Mr. Calder left us, he directed me to Lloyd's bank, where I got twenty dollars exchanged to yens and then he bade us good-by at the Imperial Hotel where he was to meet us again later.

Around the World at Seventeen

For all its mud streets, Tokyo impressed me with its beautiful and fantastic buildings. One of these, the Arcade, resembles a tunnel two blocks long, with little niches for booths, where the tradesmen display their wares. I was bewildered by the sight of all the beautiful and interesting articles one could purchase at unheard-of prices, such as high-grade Japanese porcelains, lacquer and bamboo wares, silk and embroidery, kimonos, brocades, cloissoné, damascene, fancy matting, all kinds of braids, toys and ivory inlays. There were included in this unique emporium, many other excellent shops where one could purchase both Western clothes and Japanese garments.

A word about the dress of the Japanese gentleman of the present day. Above all, he prefers a straw hat, winter and summer. An odd sight is a man in a heavy overcoat with a straw hat that might grace Troost Avenue on the hottest summer day. Next, he likes English shoes. His trousers are baggy at the knees and held tightly above the ankles with an elastic, leaving an inch or so of white silk sock showing above the tan shoes. If he is inclined to extreme dressiness, the trousers may be of blue satin. The sash about his waist is also blue. In fact, blue is the Jap's favorite color. He will wear a *hoari* coat, with a broad ribbon of his favorite color over one shoulder and diagonally across the shirt front, and exposed to

Around the World at Seventeen

view when the coat is worn open. The last and most important equipment of the correct-appearing Japanese gentleman is a Chaplinesque mustache.

Tokyo, exceeding two million in population, is the capital of Japan and the sixth largest city in the world. In olden times it was called Yedo, a name derived from Yedo Tedo, a general of the forces of the famous Shogun, Minamoto Yoritomo, who toward the end of the twelfth century chose the place for his headquarters. When the Shoguns were deprived of power in 1868, Emperor Mejiji removed the seat of government from Kyoto—"Western Capital"—to Yedo, changing its name to Tokyo, or "Eastern Capital." Not only is Tokyo the center of culture, and of the government, but the location of the principal universities of the Kingdom.

Mr. Mizzlewitz met us at the Imperial Hotel as arranged in his note to Paul Robinson. Government owned, this hotel is the most unique and interesting hostelry in the world, surpassing in sumptuousness anything I have ever seen. It likewise was untouched by the earthquake and fire, a fact for which there is a remarkable explanation. This great structure of Spanish type, faced with gray textone brick, rests on a floating foundation anchored to piles, which minimize the severest quakes. On entering you immediately feel the atmosphere of the place. Artistic draperies hang everywhere in the subdued light. Ex-

Around the World at Seventeen

cepting in the lobby, the ceilings are low-studded, almost within reach of one's hand. Shaded tunnels in all directions form hallways leading from the spacious lobby to the guest rooms. "Mizzie" conducted us through grotto-like passages, up dim stairs, to the roof, where we had a magnificent view of the city. There we beheld the Emperor's Palace, with a moat sixty feet wide surrounding it, and the Imperial guards slowly walking their posts. In distant parts of the city we could see clusters of factory smokestacks, belching black columns of smoke, denoting the push, energy, and indefatigable industry of the little brown race in their determination to set a pace in world progress.

We descended from the roof at Mizzie's suggestion to partake of tiffin with a number of distinguished Americans to whom he introduced us. Mizzie attended to the ordering after we were seated at a little table in a quiet nook of the tea room. Here we had our first—and last—drink of native *sake*. Bullion of fishy flavor, with cubes of bean curd floating in it, was next served in black lacquer bowls, then came a mixture of chicken, eggs and green vegetables on rice, accompanied by a small dish of brown sauce, called "soy" used as salt. We were served likewise with a saucer of sliced cucumbers and carrots of briny taste, and individual pots of pale green tea. We were asked innumerable questions as to our im-

Around the World at Seventeen

pressions of Japan by the eminent gentlemen Mizzie had invited for the occasion, and our rejoinders were either ridiculous or pointed with wit, judging from the hearty laughter they evoked.

Our plans included something more than merely putting up at a modern hotel where the service was American enough to make us feel we had not left home. We wished to spend the night at a typical Japanese inn, with neither friend nor guide to steer us into safe waters. We left the boat athirst for adventure and we were determined to find it. We proposed our plan to Mizzie and he obligingly agreed to direct us to an inn patronized only by the Japanese. Then he bundled us into a taxi-cab, gave the driver the address, and sent us on our way.

Either we looked like ready money, or Mizzie was taking no chances, for the inn to which he sent us was the most expensive and exclusive in Tokyo, as we learned on paying our bill in advance—thirty dollars for three persons in one room.

Long before we reached the inn we realized we might be doing a foolish thing. It was nighttime, and the three of us were seated in a taxi-cab dashing through unfamiliar and poorly lighted streets, turning corners in every direction, headed toward an unknown inn, and with no idea how to return to the Imperial Hotel next morning.

The taxi driver finally drew up before a long, low,

Around the World at Seventeen

building, the second story of which was tucked almost out of sight under a sloping, curved, tile roof. We got out, dismissed our taxi and entered the door which always stands open in a sign of welcome. A diminutive woman in a blue flowered kimono came forward and greeted us with the usual smile.

We were so obsessed with the idea of sleeping in a Japanese inn that immediately after the formality of paying our bill, we started up a flight of stairs to our room. The inn lady set up a chattering; a man appeared above us and blocked our way; consternation was expressed in the glances they cast at us. We knew at once we had violated one of their sacred customs; just which one, however, was not evident until the man and woman ran up and grabbed the three of us, hustling us down the stairs, chattering volubly and pointing to our shoes. Then we understood. It is the greatest insult a guest can offer to wear shoes across a threshold. It simply is not done. We replaced the shoes with little soft, padded slippers and being graciously forgiven were conducted to our room.

The rooms of even the most sumptuous hotels in the United States are niggardly in size compared to those of a good Japanese inn. Here we found spacious quarters, made to appear larger by the dearth of furniture. A hemp matting covered the floor, beautiful Japanese prints hung on the walls and became dis-

Around the World at Seventeen

cernible to our eyes as the man servant, or *boison*, switched on an overhead electric light. In one corner was a private shrine with the great god Buddha squatting cross-legged, incense burning in his folded arms. There was no stove and it was cold. The shell shutters were wide open, and these we closed immediately. We were beginning to wonder where we would sleep when the *boison* and *maison* returned, each bearing thickly padded quilts. One of these they placed on the floor, the other, of satin, was to be our cover, while for a headrest we had pillows stuffed with rice. Then we put out the lights and turned in.

The moon had risen and cast a dim glow through the transparent shell walls bisecting at intervals the narrow strips holding the shell beams in place. In the moonlight these strips were metamorphosed into bars and we could well imagine ourselves cast into prison in a foreign country. As a matter of fact there was an element of comedy in our situation. For days on shipboard we had planned big things when we landed in Japan; and here we were at seven o'clock in bed! Stranger still, we were ready for it. We were dozing off to sleep when Killick suddenly sprang up in bed with the exclamation, "Great Scott, I have an engagement at eight o'clock!" He scrambled out of bed and dressed and rushed from the room. Not long after Paul and I went to sleep.

About four o'clock I woke up and nudged Paul. He did not need it, however, because he, too, was

Around the World at Seventeen

awake. Nobody could sleep in that freezing cold room. We got up and put on our clothes and overcoats and opened the shutters. In the pale moonlight, Tokyo spread before us in silvery brilliance and somber shadows. We were cold and hungry. I never had been so hungry in all my life. There was no place to wash and certainly no place to eat and we decided to leave. We tiptoed downstairs, found our shoes, and would have sneaked out unobserved, but the same kimonoed lady was still on duty and she looked at us in amazement, no doubt thinking Americans were queer people to be out of bed at such an hour.

There we were in the streets of a strange foreign city, where the signs meant nothing to us even if we could read them, at an hour when no one was astir, and if there had been we could not understand their language. Nevertheless, we set out briskly, to warm our blood against the chill that penetrated our very bones. Presently, whom should we meet but the milkman, pushing a cart from door to door. Arriving at a customer's house he deposited a long, odd-looking bottle of milk on the door step, rang his bell and passed to the next. We attempted the sign language on him; and that failing, we kept repeating the words, "Imperial Hotel." His face brightened and he pointed in a general direction, chattering volubly meanwhile. At least we learned that somewhere ahead of us lay the hotel we sought, and we left him, visions of a hearty breakfast winging our footsteps.

Around the World at Seventeen

Through an unfortunate oversight, we had let our supply of cigarettes run out. We searched the early morning shops for American brands. There was none to be had, and we contented ourselves with sampling at least a dozen packages of Russian, Egyptian, Turkish, and native fags, only to find they nauseated us with their mildness. Finally we struck a paved street and after two hours' walk reached the Imperial.

We were literally weak from hunger and had anticipated walking into the coffee room, primed with a breakfast order that would stagger the most hardened *boison*. It was six o'clock, breakfast would not be served until seven. How the hour dragged!

Killick met us at the Imperial Hotel and the three of us returned to Yokohama. We were determined to take a bicycle trip, possibly to Mt. Fuji, "The National Mountain," worshiped above all other shrines by the patriotic Japanese. We first changed to woolen shirts, corduroy trousers and tan lace boots. Then we began our search for three suitable bicycles.

It is the bicycle age in Japan. Everywhere, we saw little brown men and smaller brown women, the latter kimono clad, pedaling them along the streets, highways, and byways. We anticipated no trouble in securing machines, so plentiful were they. Our first disappointment came, however, on being convinced that a trip to Mt. Fujiyama was out of the

Around the World at Seventeen

question. Later, our eyes substantiated the information, although, as a matter of fact, Professor Raber led a party to the top, requiring approximately forty hours to make the round trip. Not caring to encounter such hardships, we contented ourselves with planning a bicycle trip to the famous Diabutsu.

We engaged a chauffeur who spoke English, and started on a determined quest for our bicycles, after being forewarned of failure. We drove to the street of bicycle shops, got out and with the aid of our linguistic driver began our search. Killick, Robinson and I are all above medium height—indeed, Robinson is an inch or so over six feet—and as we plowed our way through the multitude, our ears filled with the clatter of wooden shoes on the pavement like raindrops on a slate roof, we felt we were giants in Lilliput. Our search turned into a routine of asking and being refused. But always with a smile. I am convinced that if a Japanese had occasion to cut off your head, he would do it neatly but smilingly.

Generally speaking, the American is the most spoiled of all globe trotters. He is known everywhere as a go-getter; and everywhere, no matter how unreasonable or freakish his demands, the least he gets is polite refusals. But two failures in one day—our inability to "do" Mt. Fuji, and secure bicycles—presaged a dull time. We dismissed the driver and walked to the Kamakura railway station, determined to make the best of a bad start.

CHAPTER NINE

The University Afloat cruise had been well advertised in Japan and the whole nation had planned a reception. It was said the Imperial Government spent sixty thousand dollars for our entertainment. When we boarded the train for Kamakura, a Japanese gentleman in Western garb came over and introduced himself in good English. He was educated at Columbia University and knew America as well or better than we knew it. I was curious to know his opinion of the Exclusion Act. His arguments were both adroit and convincing; but I was too well aware of the cheapness of Japanese labor to be converted to his way of thinking. Still there was some justice in his claim that a great race, such as ours, should not be prejudiced against another great race, such as his, because of the economic conditions in the one state, California, which brought about the Exclusion Act. There are two solutions for Japan's overpopulation —birth control or war. As there seems to be no hope of the former, the latter seems to be inevitable.

Twenty-five minutes out of Kamakura, we got a magnificent view of Mt. Fujiyama. This mountain, the name of which means "National," is the highest in Japan proper. Its perfect cone rises to an eleva-

Around the World at Seventeen

tion of 12,395 feet above sea level. We saw it streaked with snow, clear-cut although sixty miles away, superb in proportions, flawless in symmetry, and peerless in beauty. Fujiyama, which symbolizes the spirit of Japan, is idolized by the natives, and the name is stamped everywhere. Business firms incorporate a picture of it in their trademarks. It is on postage stamps, currency, paper-cutters, and bric-a-brac, as well as on the clothing of the people. In July and August, swarms of pilgrims and other folk climb its sacred summit which commands a magnificent view, that of the sunrise being markedly impressive. Two or three days are required to make the round trip comfortably from Tokyo. Stone huts, some holding two hundred persons, are available as resting places along the half dozen trails leading to its peak.

Kamakura, by the way, was the active administrative center of the Minamoto Clan during the latter part of the twelfth century and at that time had a population of nearly a million people. After the Shoguns' power was broken, the town was frequently burned by the successive warring factions and gradually sank into unimportance. To-day, its one-time greatness is reflected in the multitude of time-stained temples and shrines and tombs that occupy the many desirable sites around the ancient capital.

Still, Kamakura is a beautiful town, well worth all

Around the World at Seventeen

the time the traveler can give it. Every Japanese is an artist at heart. Perhaps nowhere in the world can be found such wonderful landscape gardening. In an overcrowded country, where space is limited, where effects of sweeping vistas and "bigness" must be created, a Japanese gardener achieves the feat with dwarfed pines grouped in tiny groves on little hills, with diminutive stone torii pointing the way. Glimpsing these parks down flower-lined pathways, the beholder receives an impression of a distant view of tree-clad mountain slopes. Every tree and stone, each of the innumerable ponds and fountains, in a Japanese garden has a meaning. For instance, there is the "Shoe Removing Stone," by the door of the humblest cottage, that in view of my recent experience at a typical Japanese inn needs no explanation. Near by is the "Sword Removing Stone," now only a reminder of feudal days. All Japanese households have their gardens, sacred and significant; and it is interesting to note that in case the owner moves to another home, he likewise moves the garden, for it is considered household property. The Japanese would as soon think of leaving behind his chopsticks and *sake* cup. Diminutive gardens fitted to a diminutive people; and in each of these somewhere under some bush a stone god sits in peaceful contemplation. November is chrysanthemum month in Japan. Nowhere else have I seen such a profusion of the yellows, whites, orchids, and reds, each blossom fluffy and soft, exquisite enough to be milady's powder puff. One can convey but dimly the sense of beauty, of peace, of other worldliness, suggested by these multitudes of flowers. The heart responds, whether one be of the Occident or the Orient.

When first I reached Yokohama I was inclined to question the sobriquet of the "Flowery Kingdom." I could not understand how plants and blossoms could exist, much less thrive, in such a forbidding climate. The floral colors in Japan lack nothing of the vividness one meets with in the tropics. It began to dawn on me why, after all, the great red sun should be emblematic of Japan. One feels the calls of romance and adventure, the air is bracing, and life is a succession of vivid colors. The fragrance in the air goes to one's head like old wine. One is happy without knowing just why, and Killick, Robinson, and I felt like colts for the first time turned into a fresh, green pasture.

In the gardens through which we progressed, we found wonderful old temples, shrines, and, most numerous of all, pagodas. The latter we found everywhere. The curiously shaped buildings which I had always thought of as summer houses, are sometimes quite large, with red tile tops, and curved, sloping roofs, and usually are surrounded by eucalyptus trees. Many of the pagodas are shops where articles

Around the World at Seventeen

of Japanese manufacture are sold to the world that comes sight-seeing. The Japanese are a frugal people, they depend for revenue almost solely upon their exports. It would be interesting to know just what percentage of our export goods are purchased in the home shops.

Our purchases included three snakewood sacred canes, curved like shepherd's staffs, and with these held at jaunty angles we made the rounds of the shrines and temples. The two principal religions in Japan are Shintoism and Buddhism, although with thorough Western impartiality we took as much interest in one as the other. Not being able to decipher the turkey track writings on the banners and signs everywhere displayed, we could only make a guess as to which particular god we gazed on in the numerous shrines. We followed the example of others who seemed more familiar with native practices, and removed our shoes, overcoats, and hats on entering the sacred doors.

The word pagoda comes from pa-god, literally a temple of a god. The Japanese pagoda differs from the type found in China. Instead of being pyramidal and eight or ten stories high, as in the latter country, it usually consists of one story only and is erected in the shape of a square, although where several are grouped together they form three sides of a quadrangle. The roofs are usually of tile, concave, creat-

Around the World at Seventeen

ing an artistic effect which is heightened on cornice and rafter by red and black lacquer work, gargoyles, devils with horns, or other grotesque images. I noticed this particularly on the Shinto shrines, where even the trees about it were curled and gnarled, trained in accord with the Japanese conception of the artistic. Irregularity of form is, of course, one of the basic essentials of all Japanese art.

But the big event lay ahead of us. We hired rickshas to transport us to the Diabutsu, the great Buddha, which we reached after a thirty minute ride. A superb, silent, elegant image, this great bronze figure has squatted with hands resting upon crossed knees before the reverencing gazes of untold millions of worshipers since 1252. It is one of the largest bronze castings in existence, measuring fifty feet in height, with a circumference of ninety-eight feet. The length of the face alone is more than eight feet and the width of the eyes four feet. The eyes are of pure gold. From the center of the forehead protrudes a wart-like knob, measuring fifteen inches in diameter, containing thirty pounds of pure silver. The image weighs four hundred and fifty tons, and its hugeness is best appreciated on learning the outer plates are only an inch thick. The visitor may enter the figure through an orifice in the right side of the lotus blossom pedestal and can climb up a ladder to its shoulder, where two small windows are placed. Two

Around the World at Seventeen

diminutive Buddhas are enshrined in the interior of the great statue. We were told that during the earthquake of 1923, the mammoth figure was completely turned around, facing again in the same position and at the identical angle it originally rested. It formerly was inclosed in a building one hundred fifty feet square, which was damaged by a devastating storm in 1369 and was finally carried away by a great tidal wave in 1494. Since that time the image has remained in the open.

I stood looking up at the symbol of a world old religion. Whatever the merits of our Christianity may be, one necessarily feels presumptuous in trying to replace this older faith with our newer one. I looked at the drawn eyes, the silly grin—there was a smug grimace on that countenance, very impressive, tremendously ugly—and as I gazed, the clouds behind, just on a level with the eyes of gold, came within the range of my vision and it seemed as if the head raised beyond the clouds into the heavens.

I was awakened from my dreaming by the recollection of an early evening engagement with Mizzlewitz in Tokyo, and we jumped into our rickshas and raced our runners to the station. We had failed to reckon on a change of stations at Yokohama. It was seven o'clock when we arrived at Yokohama and we had an hour and thirty minutes in which to rush to the boat, don our Tuxedos, return to the station,

Around the World at Seventeen

make the journey to Tokyo, and thence to the Imperial Hotel.

A taxi was our most urgent need. We burst headlong into a cab-stand, guarded by an attendant who looked at us in amazement, if not in fear. We wasted precious minutes trying to make ourselves understood, after our repeated shouts, "Taxi! Taxi!" awakened no response. Did the attendant then get us a taxi? No, the attendant did not get us a taxi. Instead, he picked up the telephone receiver, looked at the ear-piece in the manner of one examining a curious and unfamiliar object, placed it gingerly to his ear and coughed once into the transmitter. That single cough awakened a rattle and chatter in the receiver at his ear which even we, a few feet way, could hear distinctly. The attendant stood bowing and kotowing, but never saying a word while the chattering, if anything, grew more voluble. After the lecture or sermon was over, the attendant coughed once more, hung up the receiver, turned to us with the national grin and motioned us to a taxi at the sidewalk.

We missed Mizzlewitz after all. Jack Aiken had joined us at the boat and we four had a banquet at the Imperial Hotel, served by a French chef. After our feast, holding ourselves very erect and carrying our snakewood canes with military precision, we emerged from the Imperial Hotel in search of the

Around the World at Seventeen

office of the *Japan Advertiser*. By this time, we were quite experienced in finding our way about and we had no difficulty in locating it, and there we found "Mizzie," and with two fellow cruisers, Jack English and Bob Dalmeyer. These boys were old friends of "Mizzie's," the three belonging to the same fraternity in the University of Missouri.

Leaving the group chatting about 'varsity days, I wandered to a French window that opened into a tiny court beyond which was a typical Japanese living room. While standing there a geisha girl appeared in the quarters opposite and bowed and smiled effusively at me. Not knowing what else to do I returned the salutation. After a brief conversation in the sign-language, neither one understanding the other but both highly pleased, the almond-eyed maid motioned me to remain where I was, and disappeared. I waited, wondering what was to come, while the gang joked me on my conquest. The geisha girl came back holding out a photograph, pointing to herself and exclaiming, "Picture!" Not knowing what else to do I took it, bowing and smiling my thanks. I had no idea what to give her in return, so I presented her with my card. She clapped her hands, laughed gleefully, bowed, blew me a kiss and again retired, to return almost immediately with a bevy of geisha girls, all of them giggling and looking curiously at my card. A happy thought struck me and I sorted out a dozen of the pasteboards and passed them around. Then

Around the World at Seventeen

they all blew me kisses by way of thanks and disappeared to return no more.

We then turned our attention to the question of the evening's entertainment. Robinson and I were particularly keen and fresh, due to our previous night's "early to bed" policy. We adjourned to the Imperial Hotel, where we increased our crowd to eleven, with Mizzlewitz as our leader. He had maintained a mysterious silence during our discussion, and now advanced the information that he had acquired title to the "Silver Bell" for the night. Then he disappeared.

Not knowing he had gone to get his car, the ten of us found a Ford taxi, into which we piled, much to the driver's dismay. Down went the tires under the overweight; up rose the driver's protests; ricksha men rushed up to aid cabby in dispossessing us, while the ten of us, wielding our canes valiantly, fought them off. The commotion had reached the danger point when "Mizzie" drove up in his car, placated the irate driver, and divided the crowd evenly, for the drive to the Silver Bell.

We drove through unpaved streets and presently came to a house with a single green light. The exterior of the Silver Bell is not worth describing; the interior beyond description. It was a combination of the Green Mill, the Club Dover and Sloppy Joe's joint in Havana. The proprietor, dry-washing his hands, bowing and smiling, informed us the place was

Around the World at Seventeen

ours and we proceeded to take possession. We steadied our equilibrium with the best ham and eggs I ever had. I should say the best half dozen eggs and ham, for I am sure every one of us consumed that many. The ham was of just the right thickness, well cooked and juicy, and was cut in circular form to fit the plate; two fried eggs cooked in the shape of a half moon rimmed this delectable dish and our choice of drinks was unlimited. A bevy of geisha girls danced the quaint Japanese dances. In return Jack Aiken danced the Charleston, much to the delight of all present, including the geisha girls, who expressed their glee by clapping their hands in time with the syncopated music. Jack Aiken later danced the Charleston at the command of both the King of Siam and the Queen of Spain. One of the amusing stunts during the evening's entertainment was to pick up a diminutive geisha girl and toss her from one boy to another, to the accompaniment of her excited screams and laughter. These girls, by the way, occupy very much the same position as our professional dancers; they come from good families and their artistic training begins in babyhood.

We returned to the Imperial Hotel at three o'clock in the morning and settled ourselves in chairs for a short snooze, in preference to paying five dollars each for a bed. It was so near time to entrain for Yokohama that any attempt to sleep was hardly worth while. I don't remember who suggested the idea, but

Around the World at Seventeen

ten active fellows are not going to sit in chairs and wait for something to happen. The first we knew, we were out in the patio garden in the cold, crisp air, overcoats thrown aside, and tuxedos tightly buttoned, going through the manual of arms and drill steps under the command of Jack Aiken, drill master. All of us had had military training. We were exhilarated by the chill air, and to us the precision of our "right dress!" and "fours right" excelled anything ever pulled by a crack German guard. We soon had an audience of ricksha men who were gathering for the early morning traffic, and the sleepy servants came out to eye us in astonishment and remained to laugh, wondering no doubt what stunt the crazy Americans would pull next.

During these exercises none of us showed any signs of fatigue, but, believe me, when the four of us climbed aboard the first train to Yokohama, we stretched out on the seats, laid our canes across our breasts and fell asleep. By vigorous shaking the conductor managed to awaken us on our arrival at Yokohama. We had planned to hurry to the boat, change our evening clothes for street dress, and join our section for a trip to Nikko; but passing the Tent Hotel we decided we must eat, which we did largely despite the unearthly hour. The delay this occasioned, brought the realization that we would never make the boat and train too. We decided not to change, hiding our evening clothes by buttoning our over-

Around the World at Seventeen

coats close about us, lest we be detected by the professors. In this garb we hurried to the station.

We were dead for sleep, tired from dancing and frolicking. In the cold gray dawn of another day the thrills and pleasures of the previous one were forgotten. To climax our depression, just as we came in sight of the station, we saw the Nikko train slowly pulling out.

We were galvanized into action, and forthwith sprinted after the train at a rate of speed creditable on any cinder track, waving our canes and shouting to attract the engineer's attention. He looked around at us, grinned widely, and gave the throttle another yank. The train moved forward with increasing speed, the four of us in hot pursuit, neither gaining nor losing ground. No hundred yard dash ever thrilled a grand-stand of spectators as we thrilled the passengers of that train. We forced our feet into a final sprint that slowly, then more rapidly, diminished the distance between us and the rear platform. A final gasp, a desperate leap, and neck and neck we hooked our canes over the platform rail and, sputtering and grunting, scrambled aboard. We had made the boat!

The next moment we looked at each other in disgust. The train slowed down and finally came to a dead stop at a signal tower; and there it remained for fifteen minutes while a long freight train rumbled past on an intersecting track.

CHAPTER TEN

ON the journey to Nikko, we passed the time discussing the scenery along the way. We were traveling due north from Tokyo, passing through the heart of the agricultural district, and the further north we went the thinner grew the population. We passed neat little farm houses, vine-clad and made colorful by foliage and blossoms, tucked in the midst of persimmon groves. Vistas of long lanes came and went; bicycle riders pedaling up and down them. There is something about rural Japan that reminds one of England. The farms are green and the villages clean and in good repair.

After an hour or so we began to see mountains in the distance with trees leaning from their sides. Everywhere, the lanes were shaded with eucalyptus trees, fifty feet high. Finally, we entered a canyon where the verdure was like that of spring, and the mountains precipitous and rugged. At last, we arrived at the valley station of Nikko.

Nikko, meaning sunshine, is situated in a little valley with mountains rising all about it. Five hundred strong, the cruise swarmed off the train and rushed over to the eight waiting street cars, which were to transport us to the shrines. For some reason the con-

Around the World at Seventeen

ductors and motormen had not put in their appearance. There were about sixty-five passengers to the car. They were tiny little contraptions, never intended to hold such a mob and we were impatient to be on our way. It was bitter cold and, to warm up, several of us began running back and forth from one end of the car to the other. These cars travel on a pair of trucks placed beneath the center section. If the load at one end were heavy enough it would lift the other end like a seesaw. The moment we discovered this natural phenomenon, we began playfully tilting one end and then the other, to the accompaniment of shouts and the clanging of the gong. The other cars followed our example and the surprised beholders saw a sight resembling a western rodeo with eight bucking broncos, sun-fishing and buck-jumping all at once.

When the car men arrived order was quickly restored and we started up the street, which was so hilly that it resembled the surface of a shoot-the-chutes railway track. We would hang breathlessly at the summit, plunge down a hill with breath-taking speed, and slowly climb the next, repeating the performance endlessly. While we were doing this we were passing along a street so narrow that carts, in order to let us pass, darted into doorways for safety. Indeed, one could almost reach out either side of the car and touch the walls of the buildings. From these doorways of

Around the World at Seventeen

tiny shops, Japanese men, women, and children, waved and shouted, "Hello, Americans!"

We progressed in this manner to a junction of streets, one of which was the famous Cryptomeria Avenue that stretches for twenty miles, I was told, lined all the way with huge trees. Here the street railway terminates and on foot we began to ascend the hill of shrines, a winding, dirt street, narrow but fronted on either side by the most wonderful shops I ever beheld. These shops are famous for their marvelous lacquers, trinkets, puzzle boxes, vases, cloissoné, and inlay work. Mere glimpses into these tiny treasure houses made me think what could I not do with five hundred dollars!

We were climbing steadily up a grade quite all of forty per cent. There were many who rode in rickshas with their coolies puffing and blowing and straining in the shafts. Robinson, Killick, Aiken, and I preferred to walk. Despite the fatigue of keeping on the go more than twenty-four hours, we felt the need of exercise to alleviate the biting cold. Our canes earned their purchase price on this climb!

Finally, we arrived at the shrine gardens, which covered the steep ascending hill, heavily forested with tall, slick bark trees, many of which I am sure were one hundred feet high. The first of the shrines was at the foot of a stairway which ascended for a quarter of a mile the steep slope of the gardens in a series of stone flights. Here we removed our shoes. The two hundred pairs of every conceivable shape and size, marshaled in orderly rows, reminded one of the "footsteps in the sands of time." There were no slippers to replace our shoes and the cold, biting into our stockinged feet, added to the natural embarrassment of many who had left their darning kits at home—especially the girls.

In the shrine court-yard we saw the three sacred treasure houses, surrounded by little posts mounted with lanterns of carved gold. There was little of interest to see to an Occidental unversed in the sacred lore of Shintoism. Naturally, in the sacred precincts, conversation was limited to whispers and there were no guides to enlighten us.

Every one marveled at the greenness of tree and flower, in view of the intense cold. Perhaps the verdure made all the more striking the weather-beaten and faded colors of the shrines. The exterior of the Holy of Holies had a bright, fresh appearance, due to the predominance of gilt and gold and silver inlay work. Yet, no one dared indulge in the traveler's natural passion for souvenir collecting.

The Holy of Holies has one chamber which the Emperor himself is not permitted to enter, but the three brass images which comprise the principal shrine may be seen and worshiped by all. Over their

Around the World at Seventeen

heads hangs a tapestry extending the full length of the main room and woven from pure gold.

The cruise was divided into convenient sections and as our section progressed up the stairway we met other sections coming down. Up and up we mounted. After a while with our endurance at low ebb, we received the encouraging information from those who had gone before that there were only two thousand more steps to climb. To our relief, however, we made a final right turn, and came suddenly upon the topmost shrine. Here we tarried for a moment to rest and purchase a "luck slip" from an old priest—the only evidence of graft we had encountered. Our feet were almost frozen and we returned quickly to our shoes, hurried back down the sloping street, paused long enough to make a few modest purchases in the marvelous shops aforementioned, and then we boarded the train for Yokohama.

The *Ryndam's* six days' stay in Japan was to be divided equally between the ports of Yokohama and Kobe. With three days already put behind us, we cast off from Yokohama at eleven-thirty. I regretted leaving land again, despite the strenuous activities through which I had just passed. Studies were not resumed during the thirty-six hour run to Kobe, owing to the time being taken up with mass meetings and conferences relative to the regrettable behavior of some of the cruise members in Tokyo. As none

Around the World at Seventeen

of my crowd was concerned with the deplorable episode, I will not mar the pleasant memories of my travels by setting forth the facts. Anyway, certain newspapers in the United States at that time gave the incident more airing than it really deserved.

When we docked at Kobe it was raining. No gentle shower this, but a driving, bitter-cold downpour. I had no umbrella but I donned my raincoat, and, with Killick and Robinson, left the boat. My first impression of Kobe was anything but pleasing. The ricksha men, shop-keepers, laborers—in fact every one who was unfortunate enough to be abroad —had laid aside their dry-weather sandals for the wooden shoes, and their clatter upon the board walk sounded like a stampede of the thundering herd.

The cruise was scheduled to go by rail to Kyoto, but we had other plans in view, so we hailed three rickshas. The rain had not abated; the tops of the rickshas were up, the coolies dressed in big umbrella hats and slicker capes thrown over their shoulders. As I mounted to the seat my man pulled a rubber tarpaulin over all of me but my face and buttoned it on each side of the seat back. In this position, with the raindrops pelting on my unprotected face, I felt rather like the negro target at an egg-throwing contest. Thus we drove to the Oriental Hotel.

Located on the Bund, overlooking the picturesque and animated waterfront of Kobe, the Oriental Hotel

AUDIENCE GIVEN BY THE KING AND QUEEN OF SIAM

Around the World at Seventeen

stands a monument to Japanese progressiveness. We had no intention of putting up there; however, we had no sooner entered the lobby than we were approached by Mr. Y. Shimada, who proffered his services in a pleasing manner. Later we learned he was the managing director. When we told him of our intention to make a bicycle trip to Osaka, and perhaps pedal on to Nara, he threw up his hands in dismay. It had never been done; it could not be done; the people would think we were crazy if we even attempted such a trip. Then he advanced one objection after another. Could we ride bicycles? Like natives, I replied. But we could not find our way, he remonstrated; there were neither mile posts nor signs to direct us; the roads were bad, when there were roads, and we perforce must pass through several *eta* colonies.

What was an *eta* colony? we asked; and he told us that they were the social outcasts of Japan—men who had surrendered under fire in war time—a dangerous, surly folk. They gathered in villages of their own because the women and children must share the disgrace of their husbands and fathers. According to Japan's ancient code of warfare, the soldier who surrendered was a coward, too low in social status to commune with true patriots. Therefore, they were segregated and must flock by themselves forevermore.

I later learned that this story was a little over-

Around the World at Seventeen

drawn, advanced for the purpose, no doubt, of discouraging us from taking what really was a hazardous journey. The origin of the *eta* lay in the years long gone, an unsolved problem. To-day, there is no social or religious reason for the existence of the class, and it is a monument to inherited prejudice. In 1871, the great Emperor Meiji swept away all legal barriers between this class and the general citizenry of the land. Premier Tanaka found the time to entertain three members of the colony of outcasts and conferred with them on ways and means to ameliorate their condition.

Mr. Shimada's arguments, however, were both impressive and convincing. Indeed, they were so convincing that we thanked him profusely, and immediately hunted up a porter who might tell us where to find our bicycles. The solicitous manager had waved a red flag in our faces, and, literally, we pawed the earth to be on our way.

Fortunately, we found in the smiling, obsequious porter the man we sought. He knew the very place! A friend of his had a friend who knew of a bicycle shop where they had three new machines which the friend of the porter's friend was quite sure we could rent at reasonable terms. While we were gaining this information, the porter had led us through interviews with the various friends, until we finally reached the bicycle shop, and for the modest sum of $15.00 each,

Around the World at Seventeen

we secured our mounts. The wheels were new, with new rubber. They had no coaster brakes, however, and the speed was regulated by a lever grip on the handlebars. They were, in fact, such bicycles as enthusiasts of the '90's rode in America. But we were elated over our find and rolled them out of the shop for a trial spin in the crowded street.

When our troops mobilized for the World War, a scene common to all cavalry remount stations took place daily. From the range country wild horses were purchased, and the daily task of the troopers was to subdue these mustangs. Many of them had never before known saddle or bridle. Imagine a dozen troopers mounted on these sky-reaching, pawing, panicky steeds, and you will then have a conception of Robinson, Killick, and myself mounting our bicycles for the first time. Neither had they before known a rider, and they certainly acted the part. I was first to get my bicycle balance, due to the fact that not many years had passed since I was a practiced rider.

Not so Robinson and Killick, especially the latter! Killick deserves a chapter all to himself. Aside from the fact that Robinson was six feet three and the Japanese bicycles are built for riders of three feet six; aside too from the necessity of his knees pumping up and down outside the wide-apart handlebars, he accommodated himself gracefully to his vehicle.

Around the World at Seventeen

Once in passing through Oklahoma, at a little bush league station where we made a brief halt to unload a dozen eggs, I saw an Indian buck fitted to Robinson's measurements seated on a new saddle on an Indian pony. Evidently it was his first, and the stirrups were adjusted for a five-year old. He sat with his knees thrust up alongside his ears—a very natural position for an Indian and one quite common where the shady side of a building is convenient for him to squat and watch the world go by. Robinson reminded me of that Indian.

The street was dense with shops and for every shop there was a dozen grinning, cackling Japs, who thoroughly enjoyed and appreciated the fine exhibition. But Killick was the mysterious Rider of the Purple Sage—or rather tea shops. He was a mysterious rider because he failed to inform us that he had never before ridden a bicycle. What he lacked in proficiency he made up in nerve. His face glowed with grim determination as he swung into the saddle. Like an arrow he darted across the street, headed straight for a *sake* stand. Not deviating an inch and pumping for dear life, he leaped the curb and, amid the shrieks of the scattering crowd, dashed into the shop. There was the crash of breaking bottles, a shower of *sake*—and Killick preferred it the least of all liquors. He pacified the shopkeeper with a handful of coins and determinedly took a fresh start. His next effort was

Around the World at Seventeen

directed against an innocent fruit stand which he succeeded in demolishing without half trying. He was encored for his agility and grace with a shower of carrots, potatoes, and rutabaga bouquets. Again he rained coins upon the quacking proprietor. If one plays the game one must pay. By this time Killick was almost broke and he decided discretion was the better part of valor. With great caution he removed his bicycle from the scene of devastation, placed it squarely in the center of the street, headed toward Osaka and again swung into the saddle. The street was clear—for a reason readily understood. In the distance a kimonoed lady went peacefully about her business. But not for long! Suddenly, without a thought of the pursuing white devil, the front wheels of Killick's projector caught her unaware, and she described a graceful parabola, right oblique, while Killick gave an exhibition of a dry-land dive to the left.

I am ashamed to say we did not pause to assist the lady but pedaled furiously up the street, with Killick somewhere in our rear, striving manfully to overtake us. This he managed to do after we had passed the danger zone.

CHAPTER ELEVEN

WHEN Mr. Shimada was convinced that he could not dissuade us from making the trip to Osaka, he gave us a slip of paper with the question written in Japanese, "Which way to Osaka?" In view of subsequent events we regretted it did not read, "Give us something to eat." With this as our only guide, we fled from the chattering street crowd, and rode along a seemingly endless, narrow street, with the shop men quacking and laughing at us.

About four o'clock, we reached the city limits and struck out on the paved road which we knew led to Osaka. I was voted leader, for no particular reason save perhaps a more recent acquaintance with a bicycle. The responsibility required some courage as I had no more idea about directions than the others.

Having found our way out of Kobe, we felt most of our difficulties were past. The Japanese follow the European custom of turning to the left, and owing to our habit of keeping to the right, we got into a traffic jam almost every block, dodging street cars, taxis, bullock carts, rickshas, and hucksters. But once on the wonderful new concrete highway between Kobe and Osaka, we congratulated ourselves on our

Around the World at Seventeen

achievement and felt we had already won our destination.

For an hour, we pedaled without bumps or troubles, our road clear and smooth before us. But all dreams must end—a new bridge was in process of construction. This called for a detour, and we struck out across a canal bank little wider than a street car track, with only a dim footpath for a bicycle trail. In the light of the November evening, a picturesque scene spread before our eyes. On the one hand, loomed the massive concrete spans and abutments of a modern highway bridge; on the other, sloping fields rising in billowy hills marked the rice paddies of the diminutive Japanese farms. At the bridge, technically trained engineers worked expertly with modern machinery; on the farms, the husbandmen labored with primitive plows drawn sometimes by bullocks, at others by a bullock and the farmer's wife. In the background small Japanese bungalows looked like doll houses. As far as the eye could behold, farms dotted the mountain slopes. On the horizon to the west, the tall chimneys of a factory sent up clouds of smoke, testifying to Japanese progress.

The steady upward climb, the soft dirt trails, called for our utmost exertion, and soon we suffered from cramps. We dismounted and pushed our bicycles up a three mile hill. We passed native bicyclists, coolies coming from work, and now and then a woman with

Around the World at Seventeen

a scarf or basket on her back, in which snuggled a black-eyed, doll-faced child.

Somewhere we missed the detour back to the paved road, although we had watched closely for a turn-off. At sundown we came upon a fork in the canal path. We stopped here to watch the sunset, which was different from any I had ever beheld. The impression was heightened too by the strangeness of our surroundings, the sloping farms and mountain background. Workmen now passed us in numbers; and bicycle lanterns flickered like fireflies in the gloaming. We decided to take the right-hand path, and pursued our way accordingly. Darkness brought home forcibly the fact that in our hurry we had neglected to equip our machines with lanterns. To the passing natives, we must have appeared like the headless horseman of Sleepy Hollow fame, looming as we did in the glow of the passing lanterns, huge in stature and strange in dress. This surmise was borne out by the behavior of the natives, who gave us a wide berth in passing.

It was now full night. I was in the lead, Robinson a wheel's length behind me, while somewhere in the blackness we could hear Killick puffing and grunting —in good English. Suddenly, the latter hailed us and we stopped. He had been overtaken by an old woman on a bicycle, to whom he positively had made known our need of lanterns, and who volunteered—

Around the World at Seventeen

by signs—to conduct us where they could be purchased. Our elation was unbounded; likewise our admiration for Killick's mastery of the sign language. But our joy was short lived and our admiration quickly changed to doubt. The old lady, with her gray hair flying, took the lead. She held it. Puff and speed as we might, she gradually disappeared in the darkness ahead, to be seen no more. I would give a handful of sen to know what she thought of us.

By the time we had decided our aged guide had given us the go-by, we saw a cluster of lights off to the left, and we headed down the canal bank in the pitch dark, experiencing a shoot-the-chutes sensation. By heaven-sent luck, we landed in a dim roadway and pedaled toward what we thought must be a village. Instead, however, we came upon a group of silent shacks, eerie and forbidding, where in the interim of our approach the lights had blinked out, leaving us in darkness. We returned to the canal faster than we came and proceeded on our way.

Before we were aware of our good fortune, we once more struck the pavement, and while we were congratulating ourselves we rode through the streets of a town. No thoroughfare in San Antonio could ever achieve the crookedness and narrowness of the one through which we now passed, and it swarmed with workmen going home. Always, in passing a cluster of houses, we hoped they were on the outskirts of

Around the World at Seventeen

Osaka. But soon again we were on the highway, only to meet with another detour after a fifteen minutes' ride.

The moon rose, shedding a dim light on the surrounding country, if anything adding to our confusion. It was now 8:30, we were hungry and thirsty; we had left the Oriental Hotel dressed in our boots, corduroys, and woolen shirts. An ever increasing elevation carried us into overcoat weather. Alone, in a country where we had no knowledge of the language and where the rural population was bitter against us by reason of the Exclusion Act, we might well consider our predicament a question of life or death.

In this frame of mind we rode into the environs of a town, lighted streets stretching away. This surely must be Osaka, a surmise further strengthened on turning into a long street with the shops ablaze with lights. Lanterns were strung in clusters everywhere and thousands of people milled about in the street. We clanged our bells to clear a passage, but the people only looked at us stolidly. Our appearance was such that they had the right to think what they would. We discreetly dismounted to avoid being conspicuous; and immediately a curious crowd closed about us.

Until now the slip of paper asking directions had failed to serve us. We held it up for inspection and a

Around the World at Seventeen

young Japanese came eagerly forward, bearing under his arm what we soon learned was an English reader. We asked him if he could speak English. Oh, yes, indeed! He proffered us his book as proof. We opened it and read, "I see the cat."—"Can the cat see me?" In the face of this rather discouraging evidence of his linguistic ability I launched into a further explanation of our need for lanterns and direction to Osaka. Evidently he thought we were telling him an English joke, for he ha-ha'd until he grew weak. The crowd joined in and the street and shops echoed to their laughter. The more we tried to assure him the matter was no joke the more he laughed. Finally, we shook hands with him, clanged our bells, and pedaled away.

Once past the densest crowd we began to look into the shop windows. In one of these, scarfs of brilliant hues attracted our eyes; we were cold and longed for warmth. We entered the shop, made known our wants by signs, wrapped our purchases about us and made our exit before a crowd gathered. Blinded by the hanging colored lanterns we rode for six blocks, only to find that we had completed a circle. Taking a fresh start, however, we managed to get out of town and back on the usual canal bank, riding down side alleys and through the brush.

By this time, it was 9:30. More lights loomed ahead. We stopped for a moment to tighten our

Around the World at Seventeen

handlebars before entering the village. From the behavior of the villagers, I am quite certain we were the first white men they ever saw. Here the shops were not more than five feet high. On the outside of one, a Tansan water sign invited us and we were further inveigled by a shelf of bottled water, discernible through the thin paper walls of the shops. We entered forthwith and called for Tansan. The proprietor, with eyes wide and mouth agape with awe, merely stared at us. Doubtless an apparition of white devils was foreign to his vision. As he stood there too dazed to utter a sound, our glances swept our surroundings. The shelves were cluttered with paper packages bearing Japanese trademarks. There was a low counter extending across the back. In front of it the storekeeper's wife and baby huddled over a typical Japanese stove, which was a brass opium bowl containing a live coal fire. The woman frequently replenished it from a tiny sack of charcoal with a pair of tongs.

Despite the shock of our appearance, the storekeeper had the good grace to invite us to warm ourselves while he was endeavoring to ascertain our wants. We accepted the invitation with alacrity. The ceiling was so close to the floor that really there was no need for our crouching lower than we already were, to huddle about the brass. In our gratitude we proffered the man a cigarette. It is a well-known

Around the World at Seventeen

fact that tobaccos of American manufacture are preferred above all others the world over. Already we had observed the magic effect of our cigarettes. This man perhaps beheld in us his first Americans, but judging from the speed with which he reached for the cigarettes, he was acquainted with our brands. There is comfort in the thought that while the world at large may not like us as a nation, it most certainly has a leaning toward our products. The shopkeeper made signs that his wife would like a cigarette and forthwith she was accommodated. Another man came forward from a dark recess in the rear—a brother, I suppose—and he had to have one. By this time we had grown friendly, illustrating the universal bond of fellowship between smokers, and we sat down in a circle around the fire. In answer to our signs for a drink of water the shopkeeper produced a bluish bottle, but one smell convinced me he was on the wrong trail. I rose and took down a bottle of Tansan water; then he understood, produced three glasses, and from a receptacle near by took a handful of queer-looking, queer-tasting roasted nuts. With these serving in lieu of pretzels we drank a half dozen bottles of Tansan. Meanwhile, a glance at the transparent shell windows disclosed a watching throng with noses pressed flat against the panes, grinning and chattering. We waved at them, which pleased them immensely. The shopkeeper, either mistaking our

Around the World at Seventeen

signal for an invitation or desiring to pose before an admiring audience as a host to royal guests, opened the door and invited in ten of his friends. Killick proffered cigarettes; ten hands reached out more quickly then I can tell about it. The occasion now assumed the dignified air of a ceremony. The brother arose and solemnly shook hands with the three of us. Everybody waited, with an expectant light in his eyes—that is everybody but the Americans, who did not know what was coming. Presently "buddy" returned with a greenish bottle out of which he drank first; Killick received the bottle with due solemnity and took a big swig. We watched him closely. A slight shiver ran through his body, his eyes popped open and tears ran down his cheeks. Nevertheless, game to the last, he smiled and bowed. I was next up to the bat and barely tasted the stuff. It was terrible, a sort of cross between vinegar and ipecac. Robinson made a brave attempt to down it but failed. Everybody else drank with much gusto and the bottle was passed around again, we three politely refusing the second offering.

By this time the shop was quite crowded and I felt the need of a breath of fresh air. While John and Paul were trying to make known our need of bicycle lamps, I wandered out in the street. After the warmth of the shop, the frostiness of the night air impressed on me the necessity of a coat. At the mo-

Around the World at Seventeen

ment, my eyes lighting on a display of *hoari* coats in a near-by shop, I entered and purchased one and a black sash to hold it together. The Japanese woman who waited upon me laughed heartily as I doubled the sash about my waist with the knot tied in front. In this striking regalia I returned to the crowded shop and proudly displayed my purchase to Killick and Robinson. Needless to say, the Japanese woman sold two more coats. While the boys were gone, the shopkeeper's wife, with much laughter and chattering, readjusted my sash Japanese fashion and with a pair of scissors worked over the rough edges of the *hoari* coat. Each of us presented a ridiculous figure, a cross between a Russian Cossack and a Greek goulash. While the change in our appearance was taking place, the shopkeeper had disappeared. Ready to continue our journey much refreshed and in better spirits, we stepped outside to our bicycles. Lo and behold! there was the shopkeeper, busily fixing three new lanterns to our bicycles! Where he acquired them and what they cost, we never learned, for with many signs and smiles he made known they were gifts.

Before we departed we endeavored to learn the name of this place by pointing to the street and buildings. Smilingly the shopkeeper informed us it was "Dote." A later search on the map failed to disclose Dote's existence, and eventually we learned that "dote" means street.

Around the World at Seventeen

At ten o'clock, we bade the shopkeeper, his wife, brother, and host of new friends farewell. About one o'clock in the morning we rode into Osaka. I pause here to make an observation. Japan proper, scarcely one half the size of the state of Texas, has a population of eighty-five million people. In riding on trains and motor-busses one cannot fail to be impressed with the scores of towns exceeding the hundred thousand mark, and larger.

We had now arrived at the largest city in Japan, with a population, according to the latest estimates, of three million or more. In other words, in our great country we have two or three cities only that exceed Osaka in population. Even at this late hour—one a.m.—we rode for miles along lantern-illumined streets, lined on each side with open shops. At one of these we halted. Killick, who had broken the crystal of his watch, had it repaired at a cost of fifteen cents. After an interminable time we emerged into a double paved street and came upon a street-car line. We were too tired to ride further, so dismounted and walked until we saw a policeman. Resorting to the sign language for the hundredth time, we indicated to him our desire to sleep. He nodded enigmatically, leaving us in doubt as to whether the bed to which he escorted us was in jail or in a hotel. But we were too foot-sore and tired to care; even a jail would be welcome, if it contained a place to sleep.

Around the World at Seventeen

He led us up the steps of a beautiful modern building on top of which we observed an electric triangle, the emblem of the Y. M. C. A. On the appearance of the clerk, the policeman left us and we introduced ourselves to Mr. T. Oshida, the English-speaking secretary.

Mr. Oshida was courteous; he was voluble. He seized avidly on an opportunity to converse with Americans. In our exhausted state, his battery of questions was exceedingly tiresome. To him this was a heaven-sent opportunity to get first-hand information about every conceivable question relative to every conceivable business in the United States. He was the most complete questionnaire, the most rigid intelligence test—as well as pest—I ever encountered and no doubt our rating was set below the moron mark.

We finally learned the "Y" was filled for the night, but he graciously volunteered to escort us to a hotel. To facilitate our progress, also to quiet the human questionnaire, I placed him on my handlebars and led the way under his direction. With the moon in the background, the sampan fleets with their stark, bare masts packed the river like sardines in a can. We crossed bridge after bridge where we beheld views over which an artist might rave.

We arrived at a hotel and the sleepy clerk almost fell off his stool on beholding us. At that hour of

Around the World at Seventeen

the night he surely thought three devils stood before him. At any rate, he refused to give us rooms, despite Mr. Oshida's urging. However, he did change a twenty dollar bill into yens for me at a robber discount of thirteen yen or six and a half dollars. Then the "Y" secretary led us to the Dobuil Hotel where we found accommodations. This was at three o'clock in the morning. After a refreshing sleep and breakfast, we tipped a porter twenty-five cents to take us to the roof where Osaka spread in a great panorama before our eyes.

Osaka is often called the Pittsburgh of Japan, although it is several times larger than its namesake. It sprawls, a huge industrial center, along a great hilly slope—indeed its name means "big slope." It is the commercial center of the Empire, as well as the wealthiest city in Japan. Because of its numerous canals, it is known also as the "City of Canals and Bridges," some of the latter being very beautiful. Here also is situated the Imperial Mint where Japan's coins are made.

CHAPTER TWELVE

AFTER satisfying ourselves with a view of the great city from the roof of the Dobuil Hotel, we took the train back to Kobe. We checked our bicycles in the baggage car; and in this manner, in an hour and a half, returned from a trip that had required twelve hours to make. This second day in Kobe was spent in resting, rubbing liniment on our sore muscles, and lounging in the Oriental Hotel. The monotony of the day was relieved by billiards, and at night the members of the cruise gave a big dance in the spacious Oriental ball-room.

On the morrow, we were scheduled again to make the rounds of another million shrines—for surely already we had gazed upon that number. My heart was not wholly ungladdened by the fact that our visit in Japan was coming to a close. I was tired of rickshas and every new shrine meant only another place to take off my shoes. The rickshas would still be with us in China, but no further West. The shrines, I later learned, like the poor were ever present, not only in the Orient but in continental Europe. After all, America is the only shrineless land of sunshine.

On our trip to Nara, which was to be one of the

Around the World at Seventeen

last important sight-seeing events in Japan, the Imperial Government made a very gracious gesture. Students from the universities at Kobe were detailed to act as guides on our group trips. All Japanese are Anglo-Saxon mad; American and British standards and methods are met with on every hand, and very often improved upon. Killick, Robinson and I drew two of these Anglomaniacs.

I do not wish to call them pests exactly, for their sincerity and desire to serve us were beyond question. But they supposed that inasmuch as they were interested and well informed in matters pertaining to America, we likewise would be equally well posted and informed on their country. They did not realize that a six days' visit to Japan covers only an insignificant portion of an eight months' trip around the world. Peering at us through their big tortoise-rimmed glasses, they shot question after question at us. If I chose to live in Japan I would be an optometrist. It is beyond doubt the most lucrative profession in the Flowery Kingdom. I exaggerate but slightly when I state that all Japanese students and professional men wear glasses. My second choice, I think, would be vender of American cigarettes. The slogan, "They satisfy," is as well known in Japan as at home; and any one who has smoked the various Oriental tobaccos can well understand their preference for our brands.

Around the World at Seventeen

While we plied our two students with cigarettes they plied us with questions. The new generation of Japanese pride themselves on their high moral standard, and these two exponents of virtue smoked our cigarettes with a furtive air, while they kept a weather eye out for signs of their preceptors. Between questions and smokes, they explained in detail the landscape, including the rice paddies, the farmhouses, and even the trees and rocks—why they were there, what they were for and what they symbolized to your true Japanese. Utility comes first with us, while the Japanese lay stress on the artistic. After three hours of this enlightening conversation the train pulled into the station on the outskirts of Nara.

A thousand years ago, Nara was the capital of the Empire for a scant seventy years. During this time it became the cradle of the nation's arts, crafts, and literatures, and to-day many rare old treasures are found in the city of "level land," the literal meaning of Nara. On disembarking from the train we wondered where it got its name. To reach our destination, Nara Park, we were forced to climb a steeper hill than the one we negotiated at Nikko. It is level land, you might say, set on edge.

We began our climb to the park just at noon, grumbling because we were forced to exert ourselves in our hungry state, with lunch delayed two hours. Most of the girl members of the party rode up the

Around the World at Seventeen

steep hill in sedan chairs, carried by coolies, fore and aft, with the shafts consisting of long, springy, bamboo poles which made the occupant bob up and down like a cork on the water. Not until later did I experience the discomfort of this mode of transportation.

Nara Park, sometimes called the "Fontainebleau of Japan," contains some twelve hundred acres, in which area browse thousands of sacred tame deer. At the entrance to the park, towers a great five-story pagoda, unique in Japanese architecture because of its height, watching over the millions who make pilgrimage to the shrines within the sacred precincts. Here for the moment one loses sight of the usual diminutive landscaping indulged in by the Japanese artist because of limited space. Given a thousand acres in which to express his ideas, the landscape artist need not resort to miniature trees, ponds, torii, and parkways. Giant oaks and superb specimens of cryptomeria stand beside the entrance. Here, too, we found the freak tree of nine varieties growing from one trunk. The spreading oaks were reflected in the surface of the ponds, which mirrored the inverted image of the sacred deer which stood and gazed at us incurious and unafraid.

Passing further into the interior of the grounds we encountered scores of natives—smiling old ladies, vivacious school girls, laborers in their Sunday best—all intent upon their visit to the shrine; and above

Around the World at Seventeen

their subdued chatter sounded the unceasing scraping of wooden shoes along the gravel pathways.

In the heart of the sacred park, we approached the great Kasuga shrine, fascinating both in appearance and tradition. A thousand stone lanterns border the road to the Kasuga—gifts of appreciative worshipers. The approach to the shrine, housed in a great red and black lacquered building, is ennobled by the towering cryptomeria trees along the broad avenue. Stately steps led us to the entrance.

Already we had removed our shoes. From the interior rose a din of voices and tom-toms. It was the first touch of the Orient's much-talked-of mysticism. We learned that a festival was in progress and that the ceremony we were about to witness would continue until midnight. We had given the slip to our Anglomaniacs; otherwise our voices would have grown hoarse with a reiteration of "How interesting!"

In the large square audience room, a group of natives squatted on the floor eating dried fish and drinking *sake*. In the center of the circle danced five girl attendants of Kasugahime. The immobility of their faces and the grace of their postures contrasted strangely with the weird music and hysterical shouts from the squatting priests—sounds very similar to those wrung from the Hopi medicine man in the Dance of the Green Corn. We were given to understand this racket would keep up for hours. We watched the performance until its monotony drove us away. Before we left, however, a number of the cruise made effective use of their kodaks, much to the officials' displeasure judging from their glances of disapproval.

Again outside the sacred Kasuga shrine, with our shoes where they would do the most good, we wandered into the park. Suddenly a wild shout arose. On a little promontory, we saw a native keeper, in *hoari* coat, with white pantaloons showing above sandaled feet, and a traveler's plaid cap in his hand blowing great blasts on a bugle. His blasts and shouts reached every nook of the park. As if a hurricane of wind swept from the bugle over the underbrush, branches shook, leaves trembled, and there burst on our astonished gaze thousands of deer, scurrying from their peaceful retreats, pushing and crowding about the bugler, impatient for their feeding.

For a trifle, I bought a bag of biscuits, a favorite food with the deer. I was ravenously hungry myself and am frank to confess had the biscuits been more appetizing the deer would have gone hungry. As it was, I stationed myself near the keeper and fed them to the animals. The scene might have been a deer hunter's dream come true. Pawing at each other, climbing onto the backs of their more fortunate fellows, the rearmost deer pressed about me in a close

Around the World at Seventeen

circle. I have heard it was dangerous to tease these animals; that while their horns never threaten, their sharp, cloven hoofs have been known to tear garments to shreds, and even to injure visitors. This fact was brought home to me when a big buck slashed out at me with his forefeet, barely missing my shoulders. It was then I decided I had had enough and retreated to safety.

We next paid a visit to the Great Sacred Bell of Nara that hangs in a one-story pagoda, the roof of which, in order to accommodate the bell, is forty feet from the ground. This pagoda was one of the Seven Great Temples of Nara, known as the Great Eastern Temple. The great bell, many tons in weight, is of iron casting, the inner side reënforced with a layer of steel several inches thick. A log twenty feet long hangs suspended by two sets of ropes which hold the unique clapper in a horizontal position. To strike the gong, one pulls the butt of the log away from the clapper by means of a rope dangling within reach. The priest in charge exacts a price of ten sen to boom the bell. First, I tried it and the bell gave forth a deep, rich tone; but I failed to make the bell itself vibrate noticeably. Killick next tried his hand, with little better results. Then Robinson, who was much larger than either of us, gave a mighty pull and we saw the bell quiver.

But we were not yet satisfied. Several professors

who were looking on suggested the three of us get together. I jumped up and lifted my feet off the ground; Robinson gripped the rope just over me, and Killick, being the shortest, came last. In this wise, we swung the log back, back, back, as far as it would go. Simultaneously we released it. The log hurtled with tremendous force against the bell. The huge matrix rocked under the impact and gave vent to a roaring boom that forced us to clap our hands over our ears. The priest said it could be heard ten miles or more.

Our next visit was to the Diabutsu-den, housed in a huge double-gabled temple just beyond the sacred bell. The Kamakura Diabutsu is a huge affair but the colossal bronze image of Buddha which we now beheld was the largest and oldest in Japan, measuring eighty-five feet in height and dating back to A. D. 749. In general details, it is similar to the one in Kamakura.

Every one's thoughts turned simultaneously to a belated luncheon, and a general stampede started up the hill to the charming Nara Hotel which is situated above the lake. As the crowd proceeded, two native guards near the hotel beckoned the passer-by, "To the right, please!" or "To the left!" For a moment we were at a loss to discover the cause, until an automobile swept past us bearing the Emperor's son and members of his suite, on their way to the Emperor's

BOOMING THE BIG BELL OF NARA

quarters in the hotel. This was our first glimpse of royalty, and a brief glimpse it was, as they quickly swept up the knoll and disappeared through the lordly portals of the hostelry.

The builders of the Nara Hotel showed good taste in blending the Japanese architecture with that of the West. It is one of the best hotels in the entire world in point of equipment, service, cuisine, and cellar. Nor were we disappointed in our meal. Despite our hunger, which might incline us to overrate the cooking, the food and the service were unequaled.

Robinson, Killick and I still were together when, with a good hour and a half free on our hands before train time, we browsed among the shops. There are none finer in Japan. Of course, we were always thinking up some devilment. Suddenly, we beheld a shop that promised an opportunity. It had the most marvelous display of cutlery—knives, daggers, dirks, stilettos, swords, machetes, obviously of the finest materials and workmanship. We immediately assumed an air of dignity, such as experts possess, and marched through the door three abreast. The shopkeeper, squatting on a mat in the middle of the floor, beamed a welcome. We asked to see his best grade of dirks. Still beaming, he produced three weapons of exquisite workmanship. I squelched him immediately by returning mine with the remark, "No good." Much chagrined he produced another, even finer, and

Around the World at Seventeen

ran ribbons through a sheet of paper by letting the weight of the knife cut its own way. With a doubtful air, I took it from him and picked up a hunk of steel near at hand and ran the blade over the surface shaving off little curlicues. I assumed an air of dissatisfaction; the steel was not yet of a quality I desired, and I examined the dirk with an air of contempt. The man was frantic with chagrin, he took the weapon with which I had recently shaved steel and without lathering his face, shaved the beard from his temple, the blade cutting more readily than any razor. Meantime, he called in his assistants to whom he chattered the information that the three American "experts" must be satisfied.

Of course, Killick and Robinson had taken the cue and were behaving in a similar manner. Never had I seen such a furor to please customers. The shopkeeper, perspiring copiously, grabbed up a fine whet stone. Again he snatched a sheet of paper, the very thinnest tissue imaginable. The blade seemed scarcely to touch the paper and it fell apart. Still, I hid my astonishment under a guise of dissatisfaction. No longer able to find fault with the weapon, I turned my attention to the pearl inlaid case. The knife did not fit the case. The shopkeeper spoke sharply and an attendant jumped. He placed a finer case in my hands. At last, unable to find a single objection, I capitulated, and paid the victorious shopkeeper—one

Around the World at Seventeen

dollar! Killick and Robinson purchased larger weapons and paid the munificent price of three dollars each for theirs. Still beaming upon the American "experts," the shopkeeper, flanked by his two assistants, showed us to the door with great ceremony. The subsequent history of these three wonderful blades is as follows—I have mine intact; Robinson carries his on his person, and Killick finally used his to open cans with!

CHAPTER THIRTEEN

WE started at seven p.m., November 11, for the Sacred Island of Miyajima, and missed one of the most beautiful scenic offerings Japan has for the visitor, the Inland Sea. The next morning at ten o'clock, we dropped anchor some miles off the island. Miyajima means Shrine Island. As at the approach to all important places in Japan, a giant red torii rising from the quiet waters of the inland sea greets the eye. It stands before the shrine of Itsukushima and at high tide not only the red gate of torii stands islanded but the temple itself appears to be floating on the waters. This is one of the three great sights of Japan.

After a short wait, a large tender about one-fourth the length of the *Ryndam,* drew alongside to convey the cruise to the island. The cane craze was at its height and in our passage from the boat to the landing place we amused ourselves by whacking at the swarms of fish attracted to the surface by the boat.

The streets of Miyajima resemble those we encountered on our bicycle ride to Osaka. In one of the shops I spied an object that immediately aroused my acquisitive instinct—a human skull with a mumified snake coiled about the crown, its head thrust through an eye socket. The price was five dollars;

Around the World at Seventeen

nor could I prevail on the shopkeeper to reduce the figure—and I was down to less than a case-note. Thinking perhaps the dealer would change his mind on my return, I passed on to the sight-seeing.

Arriving, the members of the cruise were curious to give the Sacred Island the "once-over." There were quite unusual and special restrictions, including a taboo against dogs, gasoline, rickshas, births, deaths, telegraphs, and flappers. We could understand how the taboo might be enforced against dogs, gasoline, rickshas, and telegraphs. But in the matter of births, deaths, and flappers there was much conjecturing. In the first place the island was well populated and it was a question how the authorities managed to prevent some deep-dyed villain from slipping over a birth or two, or maybe a death. As for the flappers, we were at a loss to know the Japanese conception of them. Unfortunately, our education did not include an answer to these puzzling questions and we were forced to accept these restrictions as being operative in full.

By this time, almost every one was tired of the endless visits to shrines and it was with relief we took off our shoes for the last time in front of Senjokaku—"The Hall of 1,000 Mats"—dedicated to Hideyoshi, who erected it in 1587. Thousands of rice paddles, given as offerings, were heaped in orderly piles. It must have been a day of sad memory to many of the natives, for we found them on their knees before little pieces of brass, weeping copiously. We wended our way through the temple on mats laid beside the railings, reminding one of a passage through a "piggly-wiggly" store. Winding in and out in this manner, we finally crossed a little river to the main shrine. A pause here, and we hurriedly retraced our steps to the lunch awaiting us.

Much the same as in any other "campus," the college spirit was expressed at various times by various crazes or fads. There was the cane craze, for instance, the mustache craze, and the sticker craze. The latter flared up at every new port, where a great rush was made to secure hotel stickers with which to plaster baggage. Returning through the park, we saw a mob of the boys in the lobby of a little inn, frantically waving their arms and canes, and pressing toward some central point. Thinking perhaps there was a fight, I pushed my way through the crowd until I got a view of the foremost students, who surrounded the little clerk, grabbing stickers as fast as he could pass them out. As I was anything but interested in the sticker craze, I turned sadly away.

Killick, Robinson and I, desiring to break the monotony of the cruise lunches, went to the Hotel Miyajima. The dining-room was already packed with students, but we found a table, sat down, and gave our order to a perspiring *boison*. Then we waited,

Around the World at Seventeen

and waited. Time was growing precious if we would eat before we sailed. Every time we questioned the waiter he would smilingly say, "In just a moment!" Finally, every one else had gone; still we were unserved. I decided to make a foray on the kitchen, and succeeded in filling my pockets with knives and forks, and grabbed up three plates of victuals, such as they were, and raced back to the table. We finally gobbled our food, and at the sound of the boat whistle raced for the tender. Halfway, we encountered a large body of students, who seemed to be in no hurry; and I decided it was a good time to drop past the curio shop and make a last effort to obtain the skull. I found the shopkeeper of unchanged mind; but throwing down my few remaining coins, I grabbed the skull and dashed for the boat. The keeper followed half-heartedly but soon gave up the chase; and with all eyes gazing with a mixture of awe and horror at the thing, I proudly marched aboard.

Next day we stopped at Moji, the principal coaling port of the country. Classes were called as usual, but between lectures we watched the natives fill the coal bunker from baskets. Twelve-inch boards were laid across the bamboo ladderways up which streamed small brown folk passing buckets of coal from hand to hand with the unvarying motion of a belt conveyer. In the crowd there were many women with children strapped to their backs. It was an interest-

Around the World at Seventeen

ing spectacle, but disagreeable because coal soot sifted through doors and portholes on the breeze, blackening everything it touched. It was against the law to take pictures at Moji; nevertheless, all day long kodaks snapped busily. Despite the crude method employed, due to the cheapness of labor, this manner of coaling was much more economical than modern machinery. When the *Ryndam* slipped her anchor at Moji we bade farewell to Japan.

November 14 and 15 were spent on the Yellow Sea. Our course was northwest and it grew considerably colder as we approached China. The first night out we encountered one of our biggest storms at sea; the waves lashed the ship, and even reached as high as the bridge. There was the usual epidemic of sea-sickness, but a group of us who were immune played cards, although the waves beating against the ship's sides drowned all sounds.

The next morning we looked out upon a yellow mud-incrusted ship. Mud was everywhere, even showing on the pilot-house bridge. The Yellow Sea is full of shallows and derives its color from the fine silt which the turbulent waters keep stirred up; sandbars are frequent, and twelve hours out of Shanghai, our next port of call, the ship stuck on one of these uncharted, shifting points of danger. For an hour the engines labored and throbbed, sending shivers

Around the World at Seventeen

through the ship's hull, until finally she "crawfished" off the hidden bar.

During our stay on the sand bar, many members of the cruise were seized with a mild panic at a report that pirates were preparing to attack. This had been known to happen, where the Chinese rovers found a ship helpless and at their mercy. Such was not the case in this instance, however, and every one had a good laugh.

We looked forward to Shanghai with relief. Opened to trade in 1843, Shanghai is the meeting place of all the peoples of the East, and it is predominantly English. Incidentally, the name of the port has been made a byword the world over by the unsavory methods used by ship masters in former days to complete their crews.

When we stepped on deck to watch the *Ryndam* sidle up to the pontoon dock, we found the weather most unpropitious for a pleasant stay in Shanghai. A biting rain, mixed with sleet and hail, descended through a fog which, even at ten o'clock, gave the scene a twilight effect. In the background, loomed concrete buildings, very different from those on the wharf fronts in Japan. The pontoon dock derives its name from the pontoon causeway that separates it from the mainland. As we were docking, a Chinese band, partly protected from the rain by huge Chinese umbrellas, greeted us with a medley of sounds supposed to be music. We were given to understand that all boats were thus welcomed. At one side, two men, holding aloft long bamboo poles, gave an exhibition with Chinese fireworks—a spectacle that would have gladdened the heart of every American youngster.

As we touched the dock, we three "Must-get-theirs," looked at each other in dismay. We had just witnessed a bad omen. Two Chinese students came aboard to welcome us, indicating that, while in China, we were to be close-herded by a body of these peripatetic questionnaires. Resignedly, we followed our bellwethers to the dock.

For some unaccountable reason we failed to learn our destination, although the others of the cruise seemed to know where they were going. But so well managed were the details of our itinerary that there was no chance to go wrong. Everybody else was climbing into taxicabs, so we did likewise.

At least, we were no longer in the land of pigmies, for the Chinamen we encountered on our drive measured well up to Western standards. Perhaps their height was emphasized by contrast with the Japanese. Everywhere the British influence was in evidence—buildings solid and massive, with that sturdy air of English permanency; signs written both in Chinese and English; streets with good old English names,

Around the World at Seventeen

such as Queen's Road and King Edward VII Street.

As this was a British port the administrative department, likewise, was of that nation. At the intersection of busy streets stood tall Sikh policemen, considered the most efficient "bobbies" in the world. With their white-turbaned heads, black beards, regular features, and handsome black eyes, these East Indiamen were of striking appearance, standing full seven feet in their regulation English police uniforms. For clubs they carry long rubber batons. Their word is law, and up to a certain point, they, personally, punish minor offenders. The most amusing sight I witnessed in Shanghai occurred when a Sikh bobby grabbed a six-foot Chinaman, guilty of some slight offense, tucked his head under his left arm, thus bending the wiggling culprit, and applied vigorously his rubber bologna club to the portion of the anatomy where it would do the greatest good.

As we passed through these royally named streets, we turned our attention to our driver, sizing him up, as usual, for possibilities in the way of entertainment. I sat beside him, while Killick and Robinson occupied the rear seat. It was up to me to break the ice. In dress, he was a typical English chauffeur; in physical characteristics he resembled the make-up of Lon Chaney, in the character part of "Mr. Wu," drooping mustache and all.

I turned from him to glance at the downpour of

Around the World at Seventeen

rain, and back again with the remark—"Nice day we are having, isn't it?"

"Yes," came the monosyllabic reply.

Thus encouraged, I ventured, "Pretty rainy weather?"

"Yes."

By this time Killick and Robinson were chortling; but I persevered.

"How long has it been raining?" I asked.

"Two days."

"Really!"

"Yes—to-day and to-morrow."

Killick and Robinson were ready to croak, but I refused to acknowledge defeat.

"Raining to-day and to-morrow, eh?"

"Yes."

"Where we go?" I next asked, dropping into pidgin English.

"Nanyang University."

Lord, more student contact!

"Well, old stud, how long be there?" I asked in sepulchral tones.

"Yes, now," came the illuminating response.

This information put the damper on my desire to hear more of Wu's two-syllable conversation. The joke was that it did rain the next day.

CHAPTER FOURTEEN

PRESENTLY, the substantial buildings of Nanyang University loomed before us through the downpour. Getting out of the car, we found ourselves the prisoners of three energetic Chinese students, a fate shared by the three-hundred-odd members of the student body and faculty, who either could not or did not dodge the elaborately prepared reception of Shanghai's thirty-seven educational institutions. These fellows, if anything, were worse than the Japanese. With an egotism born of the knowledge that their nation includes one-fourth the population of the entire world, they suppose that Americans, with a mere hundred odd million, should know as much about their country as they do about ours. We excused ourselves from our reception committee by dodging through the crowd, pushing on to the auditorium where we secured seats well up front.

On the stage sat the leading Chinese educators and our own faculty group, the latter showing some discomfort in their strange surroundings. Before long, Mr. U. F. Shen came out and made a twenty-minute talk on "The Basis of Chinese Civilization"—all in Chinese. We knew that was his subject because the program said so. Then another gentleman came out

Around the World at Seventeen

and translated what Mr. Shen had said. The translation was for the benefit of the more immature members of our cruise who understood no Chinese. It was interesting to watch the faces of our faculty members while Mr. Shen drove home his points in Chinese, turning occasionally to receive their approving nods. He naturally inferred that inasmuch as most Chinese professors spoke perfect English, the American professors, likewise, spoke Chinese. Many a covert grin was cast at our solons during the unintelligible speech.

By the time the translator had told us about the eleven dynasties, their works, flowers—leaf and petal—and the significance of the multitude of symbols we could find in China, most of us were in a state of coma. But we came out of our stupor when a dapper little gentleman dressed in the latest European style stepped to the rostrum and began in smoothly flowing, perfect English, "Ladies and Gentlemen—" His voice and personality immediately aroused interest. For twenty minutes he held forth on the "Relations Between China and the West," in which he accredited the Chinese with being a peace-loving people. They wanted no war; they wanted no trouble; they were self-sufficient, inasmuch as they could produce everything they consumed. His speech was not a threat of what China might some day do; neither was it a challenge to other nations. In the blandest

Around the World at Seventeen

manner possible he put over his thesis. China with its half billion people, its standing army of six million soldiers, its capability of raising an army greater than the total engaged on both sides during the World War—that China, loving peace, refused to be shackled. Great applause greeted the close of his speech. It was undoubtedly the best address I ever heard. It alone was worth my trip to China, by far better than any utterance I had heard from the Japanese.

Following the speech of Doctor Chao-Chu Wu, who was former Minister of Foreign Affairs under the Republic of China, we inspected the Chinese art exhibit. Pictures over which the cultured Chinamen might rave found me, in my ignorance, unresponsive. Their masterpieces reminded me of the Indian pictographs one finds on rocks, bowlders, and cliffs in our West. Perhaps, after all, it brought home the obtuseness, the necessity for concrete illustrations, and the lack of imagination, of the materialistically minded white man.

Once again we battled a downpour of rain to gain the Oriental Hotel, where we ascended to the sixth floor for luncheon. Here we enjoyed an elaborate and expensive genuine Chinese meal. Here also one thousand Chinese students, with flowers in buttonholes, and faces aglow with eagerness to shine to the best advantage in the eyes of the American students, greeted our arrival with loud applause. The seating

Around the World at Seventeen

was so arranged that every member of the cruise was flanked on the sides by a native host. English was, of necessity, the language used. One simply must pause to admire—and smile a little meanwhile— at the persistence of the Oriental in reaching out after the ideas and ideals of the English-speaking Caucasian, even while he proclaims from the house tops the superiority of his Orientalism.

At our plates was the usual table cutlery, with chop sticks added. With the American's craving for novelty, almost every one essayed to use the chop sticks. Perhaps I desired to be different; anyway I was hungry, and I chose the implements to which my hands were accustomed in furthering the object which had brought me there.

Our three students, in some unaccountable manner had recaptured us, and they now proceeded to instruct us in the polite manner of eating Chinese food. First appeared a huge silver bowl, steaming hot, which was placed before our group. Removing the lid we found a thin, boiling hot broth floating with mushrooms. There followed a polite exchange of courtesy, each one insisting that the other fellow dip in first with his fingers. Finally I took the plunge; it was rank tasting stuff. The next course was ham done in a sugary syrup. This, too, was sickening. Then came a course of Precious Rice; a basket of

Around the World at Seventeen

Precious Nuts; and so on until we got to precious Chinese cigarettes, which must have been precious indeed, excelled as they are by the rankest American tobacco.

Meanwhile, on a rostrum at the far side of the banquet hall six Chinese speakers appeared in turn, and did their bit amidst the uninterrupted flow of table talk, the clatter of dishes, and shouts of the overworked waiters. No one seemed to be aware of their presence save myself, and religiously I applauded each speaker as he bobbed himself out. As the banquet was drawing to a close, Killick, Robinson, and I exchanged meaning glances, excused ourselves, murmuring we would see our three student hosts later, and departed. Downstairs we repaired to the diningroom and ordered American sandwiches.

Later, we taxied to the Pekin Theater and witnessed a program of Chinese boxing and wrestling, Chinese music, including a Chinese girl chorus, and sleight-of-hand performance. After the show we were in need of relaxation and repaired to the Majestic Hotel, which we entered through the back door for the reason that under an arm each of us carried a bundle of laundry. In America, there would be no trouble whatsoever in finding a Chinese laundry. With a population of a half billion potential laundrymen to draw from we saw no reason why our search should go unrewarded. After passing through five or six corridors we found a girl clerk who volunteered to relieve us of our bundles.

We spent the evening at the Majestic, which in luxury and appointment resembles a New York millionaires' club. Just before midnight Killick retired, but Paul and I kept the pace. In the course of looking for something to do we ran across Phil Harrison, a writer chap who had spent many years in China, and who likewise welcomed a break in the monotony. Under his guidance, in the next few hours, we saw more of the Shanghai night-life than the average traveler sees in a fortnight. During the evening we visited seventeen night clubs. Shanghai is the first station on "The Road South." Interesting stories were told us of the beautiful women, mostly Russian, many of them princesses and countesses, whom the political upheaval in the Land of the Ex-Czar had ruined. We were privileged to dance with many of them at a cost of twenty cents a dance. The next stop on "The Road South" is Hongkong; then comes Manila, Singapore, and Penang, in Sumatra. And here is the end of "The Road," for by that time the butterflies' wings are too badly singed to fly further.

When Mr. Harrison invited us to accompany him he told us to "sew up your pockets." The party broke up at five in the morning and we left Harrison to go aboard the boat and snatch a few hours' sleep.

Around the World at Seventeen

This was one of the outstanding nights on our whole trip around the world.

Next morning, in order to whet our appetites for breakfast, we took a walk through the Italian, French, Spanish, and Russian sections, each differing in architecture from the other. Finally, we came to the native section where we saw advertised in the stores "Special old eggs"—the older the egg the more delectable it is to the Chinese taste. Stuffed beetles also were offered as inducements to the patrons seeking savory food, and living bugs sauced over. All of this on our way to breakfast!

Educationally, there is not much to see in Shanghai on such a short stay as ours. It is a modern commercial city of a half million people, with its Bund facing the water fronts where the Chinese junks ride at anchor in contrast to the British and American vessels.

The Mexican dollar is current, silver being the standard of value in China instead of gold. Beggars everywhere; it is a legalized profession in China, and woe unto the stranger who scorns the mendicant! We had no sooner seated ourselves in a little tea room in the Old Quarter, than a swarm of these pests surrounded us. A dirtier, filthier crew I never beheld, and after amusing ourselves we finally flung them a few coins and departed. The rest of the day we spent at the Majestic Hotel, where we dined. We also re-

Around the World at Seventeen

membered to get our laundry and returned to the boat in time to leave at eleven o'clock for Hongkong, midst the blare of the same band which had greeted us and a farewell salute of the fire-cracker brigade.

As we approached Hongkong, in the southward swing of the ship's course, we encountered warmer weather. Steaming through the Straits of Formosa, on the afternoon of the fourth day from Shanghai we dropped anchor off the Island of Fragrant Streams, Hongkong. The Island, in a beautiful, crescent-shaped harbor where we obtained a majestic view of the Island of Fragrant Streams, is situated a short distance from the mouth of the Pearl River and rises to a mountain peak at the base of which the city nestles like a white gem in a royal crown. Sometimes known as Victoria, Hongkong consists of two towns. In one, live European and American merchants, in the other, the Chinese.

CHAPTER FIFTEEN

Our three days' stay in Hongkong was crowded with interest. For one thing, the monotony of eternal Orientalism was broken by a sudden and pleasing bit of old England. Indeed, in the business section of the city, one almost forgot he was in China. There were no group trips the first day and we three decided as usual, to go adventuring. Here we were in a modern British city where street cars were "trams," the "omnibuses" were double-deck; and elevators were "lifts." Our ferry and railroad tickets were furnished by the cruise, and we ferried over to the Quay fronted by substantial granite buildings, with high round-columned porticos. They all bear English signs. We inquired of a typical English "bobby" the way to the Hongkong Hotel, where we lunched. On the second floor was the "Peggy O'Neil" barroom, with a bar sixty-five feet long and a dozen bar-tenders ready to serve its patrons. Here, everything was quiet and orderly, even subdued, with nothing of the bustle and loud talking usual in the American barrooms of pre-prohibition days. In view of the fact that Hongkong is a free port, one may purchase necessities and luxuries much more cheaply than at home. Before our stay in Hongkong was ended, we loaded up for the ship.

Few Americans, on beholding a mountain, can resist the challenge to climb it. Hence, on descrying the Peak, as it is called, we planned to scale its heights, from which we were told a magnificent view awaited us. It was a stiff climb from the streets to the cable car station, and we hired three sedan chairs in order to conserve our strength for later exertions. These chairs, unlike the ones we encountered in Japan, were topless. Borne along by a tall, powerful coolie, in the bamboo shafts, fore and aft, we somewhat resembled, both in looks and feelings, three unfortunates being ridden on rails. At the station we embarked on a cable-car built along the lines of our Western jackrabbit—that is, low in the front and high behind, to offset a forty-five per cent grade up the mountainside. The ride itself was wonderful, disclosing to our view English country homes surrounded by tropical flowers and trees, nestling away in some elbow of a tiny canyon which bisects the slope. Altogether, the scene reminded me of Hollywood. As we mounted to a higher elevation the panorama broadened, disclosing more and more of Hongkong, with its population of eight hundred thousand, Kowloon across the water on the mainland, and the Islands in Repulse Bay. After half an hour of this we reached the end of the cable line and went to the

Around the World at Seventeen

Peak Hotel where, from a spacious veranda overlooking a beautiful palm garden, we gazed upon a world of ocean and islands, and bays dotted with ships of all nations.

Still we had not gained our objective, and once again we requisitioned sedan chairs, the bearers agreeing to take us to the top of the Peak—a three mile climb—for fifty cents, Mexican money, each. On the topmost rise of the Peak floated the British flag. Here we saw one of John Bull's naval stations with small guns peeping over the screen parapets. Disregarding the "No Admittance" sign, we entered the gate, bent on climbing the seventy-five foot flag pole. Killick went first, with the supple bamboo flag pole swaying under his weight. After he came down I went up, and later Robinson. After this exploit, we were satisfied to return to the Peak Hotel where we lingered over our drinks and feasted our eyes on the panorama.

On the return trip we met a Mr. Satterly, an encounter that later led to an amusing occurrence. Returning to the Hongkong Hotel, Killick and Robinson deserted us to search in the shops for scarfs. Mr. Satterly and I went to the "Peggy O'Neil," and dinner. In the early evening he and I took rickshas, riding through the streets of both the old town and the new, until time to go to an English dance at one of the clubs.

Around the World at Seventeen

The members of the cruise were there in full force. It was a formal affair—full dress; but not formal for long. There were too many Americans present, who soon did away with the formality by instituting "tag" dances. If one saw a girl with whom he wished to dance, regardless of an introduction, he tagged her away from her partner. The British gasped; not a few frowned, but the fun went merrily on. Mr. Satterly expressed his astonishment, and he was not a little dismayed when I insisted he follow our example. What! It wasn't done, old chap! But after much persuasion he finally cut in; and it was a scream to watch him, as well as the other Englishmen who spiritedly resented the Americans "hogging the show." This ended a busy day.

The next day was filled with group trips, including a forty-mile cliff drive around Repulse Bay. This bay is in the shape of a horseshoe and is bordered by beautiful estates, golf courses, and tennis courts. In some respects it reminded me of the drive along the famous Pali cliffs in the Hawaiian Islands.

Our next port of call was to be Manila, after two days at sea. The second day out was Thursday the twenty-fifth, Thanksgiving Day. It was the most peculiar Thanksgiving I had ever spent. The weather was unbearably hot. We had the usual turkey dinner with the dining-room festooned and candles burning. There were some entertainments aboard, but the heat

Around the World at Seventeen

seemed to affect every one with a feeling of lassitude. I spent most of my time wondering what the folks at home were doing.

At Manila we docked at by far the best pier on the cruise. The white buildings of the capital city of our most distant possession extend for half a mile along the waterfront. Situated on the Island of Luzon, it was first reached by Magellan in 1521. The city shows distinctly the signs of its several occupations. The native quarter, the one built under Spanish influence, and the section inhabited by the Americans, is all interesting. Here during the Spanish-American War, Dewey won glory by destroying the Spanish fleet. The Philippines, due to the many dialects and mixed bloods, are almost constantly at boiling point politically, and present problems to students of government more complex than our own at home.

We were met at Pier 7 by a welcoming committee composed of eight officials, Americans and Filipinos. Killick, ever hot on the trail of some news item, left us to seek an interview with an insurrecto chief, who at the time was creating considerable interest in the Islands. Robinson and I, meanwhile, called on Mr. Carson Taylor, the owner of the principal newspaper in the Philippines.

Mr. Taylor was preparing to make a trip of inspection to one of his cocoanut mills in the center of

Around the World at Seventeen

Luzon Island and he asked us to go along. Once beyond the confines of Manila we struck out through a rolling country, over a good dirt road flanked on each side by an impenetrable jungle. We passed several lakes, and aside from the mosquito pests which we found everywhere in the tropics, we had an enjoyable time. The distance was 125 miles, and we passed village after village with their palm-roofed huts on stilts, and brown-skinned inhabitants who ran out to watch us pass. Occasional lakes, or rather marshes, with reed grasses and water trees clustered along the edges, were encountered.

Finally, we arrived at the mill, which was closed down, however, so we did not see it in operation. Mr. Taylor talked briefly with his native *administrador*, and we departed on the return journey. About six o'clock, we began to get thirsty, and our host turned into a road that soon led us to a village with a large square building near the center. This building was made of corrugated iron, and on entering, to our surprise, we saw a modern American barroom, very Ritzy in its appointments. A negro man, looking like the leader of a minstrel show, whom Mr. Taylor addressed as "Bill," came forward to serve us. Bill, we learned on short acquaintance, was mayor and chief factotum of the village. In fact, he was the whole show. An amusing character, a former soldier who preferred to remain a big fish in a little

Around the World at Seventeen

puddle, rather than to return to his native Alabama and be just plain nigger. After quenching our thirst, we bade Bill good-by and returned to Manila.

In the evening Mr. Bennet, an associate of Carson Taylor on the *Manila Bulletin*, had us to dinner at the Manila Hotel, and later took us to the Santa Anna Cabaret. This house of mirth and jazz is supposed to be the largest in the world. It is divided into two sections, one dance floor for the Americans, the other for the natives. As a matter of novelty more visitors prefer the native section.

Due to the fact that Manila is an important Army and Navy base, the visitors' time is mostly taken with club functions and sports originated by the two branches of service. Intense heat prevents Manila from being an attractive town, for the foliage and vegetation is withered as if in an oven. The second day was spent riding around with Mr. Bennet, going over the golf course, visiting the aquarium, Fort McKinley, and looking in at all the sports clubs. Later, we had a wonderful swim at the Polo Club, in a well appointed out-door tank. And in the afternoon for the benefit of the cruise the University of the Philippines staged a snappy baseball game.

The most important social event of the year in Manila is the annual foregathering at the Army and Navy Club to hear the returns from the Army and Navy football game, played halfway around the

Around the World at Seventeen

world from Manila. We were Mr. Taylor's guests at the rather exclusive affair. All branches of the service were represented, the officers resplendent in their dress uniforms of white duck.

The Philippine Islands, by the way, are the only territory belonging to Uncle Sam where prohibition is not in force, having been voted down by both the Army and Navy. With loyalty and enthusiasm aroused to fever pitch over the possible victory of their respective football teams, one can naturally visualize the chaff and banter, the wagers and defies that passed back and forth between the Army and the Navy. Wine flowed freely all this night and not until seven o'clock Sunday morning did the returns of the game come in; a tied score.

The Lunetta is to Manila what the Prado is to Havana. It fronts the bay with a huge parkway between it and the city. Here on Sunday, thousands of people gather to witness the crowning of the Virgin of Antipolo.

The biggest kick of our visit to Manila, however, came when Mr. Bennet took us to the reception of the ministers of Japan and China. It was impossible for me to understand the names of these gentlemen but I shook hands with them murmuring a few words, as did they, neither of us comprehending what the other said, but letting the spirit serve for the letter.

Classes, which were resumed on board ship after

Around the World at Seventeen

leaving Manila, were attended with little enthusiasm because of the intense heat. We were now halfway around the world, in distance, but there lay before us more and greater sights than we had put behind. A rumor spread on board, later verified by the faculty, that the King of Siam, hearing of the University World Cruise, had extended us a cordial invitation to be his personal guests on our arrival at Bangkok. The next five days at sea were spent in speculating on the forthcoming visit and whether or not we would see King Rama VII in person. In passing it is interesting to note that he is the only absolute monarch occupying a throne to-day. Conjectures as to the king's behavior toward us occasioned many wagers.

Bangkok is the most remote port on our cruise, being forty-five days from New York. We were to be the largest party of white people who had ever landed at the port. In extending his invitation King Rama VII offered as an inducement, more sights than could be counted "on two or three hands."

CHAPTER SIXTEEN

ON the sixth day, at six in the morning, we steamed into port and anchored in the mouth of the Menam River which flows tranquilly out of what seems to be a great sand-bar lined with palms and banana trees. The sea was like oily glass; no breeze rippled the water, just sticky hot air. It was our first harbor without a mountainous background. A fleet of boats, not unlike the street car boats on the Great Lakes, drew alongside to take us to the docks, which were located at Paknam, some distance up the river. After a monotonous hour and a half on these tenders, with a view of the tropical jungle unbroken save by an occasional rice paddy, we arrived and docked before a jumble of low buildings, swarming with dark-skinned natives, dressed only in short, tight pantaloons. Naked children eyed us curiously from the throng, most of them with banana stomachs, a common affliction among them due to gorging with the fruit.

King Rama VII had improvised a train of special cars to transport us the twenty-five miles up the river to Bangkok. A short walk took us from the dock to the railroad station where we embarked on the train. Bear in mind that we sweltered in tropical

Around the World at Seventeen

heat. The coaches which we entered, had just emerged from the shop and they smelled of fresh varnish. Every member of the cruise was in his best dress, and as every one knows wet varnish and white linen do not mix well. In order to avoid such a disaster, we spread newspapers over the seats. Our weight stuck the papers to the wood like wall paper, and as a result I imagine the paint shop of his Majesty, Rama VII, had quite a task for its workmen.

There were no sides to the coaches, and we pulled out of the station at Paknam, through interminable jungle growths, broken occasionally by plantations. The time was forenoon and the sticky heat discouraged any show of enthusiasm over our being guests of a monarch. To further increase our discomfort practically half the members of the cruise were compelled to stand up. Rama VII's railroad officials had figured the seating capacity in terms of native bulk, not stopping to consider that any one of us would make at least two of the Siamese. To further add to our plight, a rainstorm blew up. It was not a well-behaved, polite rain, but a deluge. In fifteen minutes more water fell than I had ever before seen in a like length of time. A beating wind drove the downpour through the open coaches as I had seen tons of spray dash over the bow of the *Ryndam*. When we emerged from the storm our caravan looked like the "Wreck of the Hesperus."

Around the World at Seventeen

After what seemed an interminable time, although it really was a scant two hours, our train drew up to another group of low buildings before which stood one hundred or more automobiles, of foreign makes, resembling our models of twenty years ago. These cars were so small that only three passengers and the driver could be accommodated in one. Killick, Robinson and I stuck pretty close together, aided no doubt, by our recent varnish experience; but for once we drew a poor egg and were among the "drags" when the herd reached the big, barn-like dormitory of Vajiravudh College. This forbidding, mosquito-infested structure, was to be the domicile of the male members of the cruise for three nights.

It was our luck, on arriving, to find all the beds taken, but it gave us a reasonable excuse to hunt quarters in the Oriental Hotel where the lady cruisers and faculty put up. To find it, was the next move. Accordingly, we struck out along a broad road until we came to some rickshas for hire. At least our common sense told us they were for hire, although we had no way to convey our wishes to the ricksha men. Finally, we pointed down the road and climbed in. There we were without Siamese money, without knowledge of the language, and without an idea where we were going, just hoping something would turn up.

Always before we had played in luck, so why not

Around the World at Seventeen

now? Before we had gone a great way, we saw an ancient taxi and over a nearby garage a sign in English. We halted our rickshas and hailed the driver. To our relief he answered in English. We made known our predicament, showing him that while we had no Siamese money we had a supply of our own currency; and we bargained with him to pay off the rickshas and take us to the Oriental Hotel. A U. S. dollar makes two *ticalls* and one hundred *satung* make a *ticall*. The taxi driver paid our three rickshas two *ticalls* and we climbed into the ancient taxi, which in lieu of a back seat had silk sofa cushions covering a board over the springs. In this wise we proceeded to the Oriental Hotel where we ate a cheese sandwich lunch.

With a much more friendly feeling toward Bangkok, we strolled out of the hotel looking for further adventures. That my straw hat should be the cause of the most amusing incident of my world cruise may seem incredible. Before disembarking for the trip to Bangkok, we had been severally and collectively warned to wear pith helmets, the said p.h.'s to be purchased for seven dollars per. As I could see no reason why my old straw would not serve all purposes, I refrained from the said p.h. Perhaps the same fate would have overtaken it—but I am getting ahead of my story.

Killick and Robinson were poking around in a shop

Around the World at Seventeen

while I stood awaiting them under the proverbial corner lamp post, idly watching the natives amble past, and fighting off mosquitoes. A dozen paces from me stood three strange-looking men, who kept glancing at me and whispering among themselves. One of them, I might say, looked like a bad character; the other two seemed bent on changing some course of action which he contemplated. In a dim way, I sensed the action, whatever it was, concerned me, perhaps my safety or even my life. But I was not left long in suspense. Breaking away from his two companions, the third individual, whom I judged to be affected by the heat or drink—both of which I had found abominable—rushed at me, not savagely so much as triumphantly, and before I was aware of his intentions, snatched my trusty straw from my head, and beat it down the street. Immediately I was in hot pursuit, *hot* having a double significance, and I overtook the interloper about the time his two companions intercepted him. I saw they were laughing as if at a joke, and being moved to caution I refrained from a display of temper.

"What's the big idea?" I demanded, grabbing him by the shoulder and reaching for my hat. "Give me my hat!"

"No, no!" exclaimed the stranger. "I want it—pray let me keep it!"

"But," I insisted, "I need it—"

Around the World at Seventeen

"So do I—it's a pretty hat—I want it!"

I saw by this time that, despite his actions, he was a gentleman, and was moved to go slowly. His two companions, almost bursting their sides, now intervened in my behalf, and the straw once more adorned my head.

"But wait!" exclaimed the third member. "I must have a souvenir—" and he jerked the handkerchief from my breast pocket. His actions were so ridiculous that even I began to laugh and after considerable argument we over-ruled his craving for souvenirs.

Introductions passed all around and I learned they were three Englishmen prominent in Bangkok University circles. The souvenir hunter was chairman of the welcoming committee to the American students, and Professor of Social Science at the University. A second member of the trio was Mr. Jamison, the President of the Bangkok Carbonated Water factory. Wherever the Englishman is there must also be whiskey and sodas, and all over the world these carbonated water factories furnish the sparkle to the Englishman's favorite drink.

We attended the dance given at the Phya Thai Palace for the cruise. The palace was one of the pretentious abodes of the king, converted into a hotel when he tired of it as a residence. Rama VII built a new palace every three or four years, it seemed, and three or four of them were pointed out to us at vari-

Around the World at Seventeen

ous stages of our itinerary. At one o'clock we returned to the dormitory, still minus a bed. There we doubled up with three other students and sweltered the night through. My bunkie was Jimmie Bass, of Austin, Texas. I was restless and did not sleep well; my head refused to grow accustomed to the pillow. Breakfast was heralded by the most terrible fumes I had ever smelled—a combination of old eggs and stale fish. Not daring to risk such a diet that early in the morning, we adjourned to the train of cars and made the morning meal off bananas, the most delicious I have ever eaten.

There followed a ride through the streets of Bangkok, with its mixture of Siamese and British architecture. Bangkok is the chief city of Siam and the capital of a kingdom embracing 200,000 square miles, with a population of ten million. The city itself has a population of half a million. Buddhism is the principal religion, and we visited many beautiful temples and shrines. Siam is famous for its rice, teakwood, and white elephants. All the trade is in the hands of the Europeans and Chinese. The history of Bangkok dates from 1789, when Paya Tak used it as a convenient base from which to attack and overthrow the Burmese army, then occupying Siam and on his becoming king, he made it the capital of the country.

The most outstanding thing in Bangkok, aside from the heat, is the peculiarity of the native architecture

Around the World at Seventeen

and landscape gardening. All native public buildings have sloping, double-gabled roofs, rising slender and straight to a lofty point. The columns of the porticoes and verandas are either round and white with a suggestion of Doric, or are square and carved, with infinite details reminiscent of the interior of the Alhambra. The landscape gardening reminded one of a miniature doll house, with the trees and shrubs trimmed symmetrically, like green strawberries standing on their stems, or like the pompons that ornament the toe of Turkish slippers.

Following a ride through the city, we took barges to the river and visited the American hospital and a nearby rice mill. Proceeding further we came to the grounds of the grand palace and visited the Wat Arun temple. Here we found an architecture slightly different from that of the Renaissance, which began with Paya Tak in 1789. The details of the Wat Arun are too intricate to describe in words. It rises something like a Russian mosque, seventy-five feet high, tier on tier, every tier being sculptured with niches in which are carved grotesque figures. The alternate tier consists of kneeling figures, with arms uplifted, supporting the tier above, and so on, each tier diminishing in size to the dome. These various tiers form good footing and many members of the cruise, including Robinson, Killick and myself, climbed al-

Around the World at Seventeen

most to the dome to study minutely the multitude of details.

We returned to the Vajiravudh College for lunch and afterward gathered in a great horseshoe before the Throne Hall to await the audience granted by their Majesties, the King and Queen of Siam. Despite the heat we were told to wear black; furthermore we were instructed to make a low obeisance when the king and his retinue came to a halt. It was far less uncomfortable to bow our proud American necks before royalty than to struggle into the hot, conventional black. Gene Harland suggested we should give the king a rousing college yell, in view of the fact that Rama VII had been schooled at Oxford. When the king finally appeared, we made our bows. He made a speech of welcome in English, to the effect that our presence would stimulate the native students to work for higher ideals, and he hoped that our student body would glean some knowledge from the visit and depart with a broader and more sympathetic understanding of his country and people. Jim Price, president of the Student Council, responded; then we gave him our *Ryndam* yell, which pleased him mightily. Many amused comments were made after the audience was over. We naturally supposed their Majesties would appear in their glorified robes of office, when as a matter of fact, Rama VII came out dressed in a white fatigue uniform, rather rumpled and

AUDIENCE GIVEN BY THE KING AND QUEEN OF SIAM

Around the World at Seventeen

baggy at the knees, and the queen wore a gown less elaborate than many of the women members of the cruise.

Mr. Jamison, one of the friends of the straw hat episode, had invited us to dine with him at the Trocadero. His parting injunction was to bring with us three dames. This we forgot to do until the last moment; Killick, the diplomat, saved the day by a chance meeting with three girls from the *Ryndam*, whom we victoriously escorted to the Trocadero where we met our host. This dinner was one of the first I ever attended where I was hungry but could not eat. On approaching the Trocadero we looked into a softly lighted and luxuriously appointed dining room. On entering we discovered the effect of dimness was caused by myriads of bugs, tarantulas, and lizards, up to the size of Gila monsters. They swarmed about the lights and scurried over the woodwork as if they, too, awaited the feast. Our first course consisted of Skeetoline oil, which was served to us in individual bowls. Into this we dipped our hands and bathed our ankles, wrists and necks, to guard against the mosquito pests. This ceremony was repeated every five minutes. If anything, the food was ranker in smell than the Skeetoline. Drink was served in covered glasses and in drinking, one lifted the cover cautiously, imbibed, then slapped the cover on.

Around the World at Seventeen

Given a hundred guesses the uninitiated could not hit on our next move, in the hottest of all countries. We went to a roller-skating rink. Of all the imaginable forms of amusement or exertion one expected to encounter in Bangkok, a skating-rink was the most surprising. Yet we skated until two o'clock. When we finally reached the dormitory we went to bed and slept despite the mosquitoes.

The third and last day at Bangkok was spent in divers ways. Killick was off to Lopburi, where he witnessed some very good boxing; but Robinson and I pursued a less strenuous course. A dozen of us, including Gene Harlan and a number of the faculty, repaired to the Trocadero for a social "get-together."

Later, Robinson and I slipped away for a quiet session over food at the Oriental Hotel. We had been some time at our table when a tall, distinguished-looking gentleman entered, a man whose striking appearance and immaculate dress would attract attention anywhere in the world. He came over and introduced himself to Paul and me as Mr. Herot, a dealer in precious stones. It later developed that he was Singhalese, an East Indian race known for its handsome men. Mr. Herot, with his regular, dark features and wonderfully expressive eyes, was no exception. He was a Cambridge graduate, and a man of unusual brilliance. In the course of the talk which followed he took from his pocket a tissue-paper par-

Around the World at Seventeen

cel, which he opened, disclosing the most marvelous collection of precious stones I had ever seen. For half an hour he talked about them in an informative and interesting fashion. His familiarity with the gems made him careless; he insisted on our examining them, taking them in our hands, holding them up to the light, meanwhile paying no attention as to their whereabouts. He took a magnificent diamond, placed it on the concrete floor and ground it under his heel, until we thought surely the stone was ruined. When he picked it up it was unscarred, but there was a hole in the concrete floor. While we exclaimed at the perfection of the stone, he listened with an enigmatic smile. Finally he told us that it was not a diamond but paste. We then learned that the manufacturers of artificial stones had become so expert that their products could not be distinguished from genuine by many of the ordinary tests in common use. Indeed, explained Mr. Herot, diamond buyers were often taken in by spurious gem dealers; and he advised us not to buy any stones offered us in the Orient, for the reason that no dealer would offer us stones of the first water. On taking his leave, Mr. Herot pressed on us an invitation to meet him later at the Phya Thai Palace. By this time we were pretty well acquainted, and he volunteered to show us Bangkok as no white man had ever before seen it.

But for some unaccountable reason, on returning

Around the World at Seventeen

to the dormitory, we forgot Mr. Herot and his invitation, a slip by the way that probably caused us the loss of an interesting evening and a much more favorable impression of the Siamese capital. Incidentally, too, I lost an opportunity to become an affluent precious stone merchant in San Antonio, whither Mr. Herot suggested he forward me a stock of his gems to market on a commission basis.

The last day at Bangkok was equally divided between wandering about the college grounds and packing our belongings for the five-hour trip back to the boat. During the day I wrote letters home to be mailed at Singapore, and we boarded the boat and sailed just at twilight, relieved to escape from the intense heat that spread like a steaming blanket over Siam.

CHAPTER SEVENTEEN

THE only notable sights on the three days' trip from Bangkok to Singapore were the beautiful sunsets that preceded the twilight on the calm ocean, and the sea of phosphorescence, of emerald green hue, that sparkled like gems as the boat plowed through the water. The water, too, was far more beautiful than the Caribbean Sea, where we first saw this striking phenomenon. The weather was slightly cooler and the boat became more animated on our approach to Singapore.

A little over a hundred years ago Sir Stamford Raffles founded a trading post and established British maritime supremacy in the Eastern seas. Singapore, known as the "Charing Cross of the East," is the capital of the Straits Settlements, and in the direct path of the great ocean highways from Europe to the Far East. It dominates the shipping and trade of all nations, and adds a strengthening link to the British Empire. Here one finds the Chinese industrious and successful, while the proud Malays are content with a hand-to-mouth existence. Spices, rubber, and tin are the chief products. Situated on an island, Singapore lies opposite Jahore, a small kingdom ruled by a sultan with an Advisory Board composed of Englishmen. A long concrete causeway connects the island

Around the World at Seventeen

with the mainland. While it is only one degree—sixty miles—from the equator, the temperature was much more pleasant than in Siam. The *Ryndam* anchored in the bay and tenders conveyed us to the Quay, where we took cars for a drive through the city, including a two hours' visit to the Botanical Gardens.

Altogether, Singapore has little of the unconventional to offer the sightseer. It is a typical English town, similar to Hongkong, very clean, with well-ordered buildings and wide paved streets. English was spoken everywhere and the buildings and street corners bore signs which were intelligible to us.

On our trip to Jahore the cruise was divided into sections, one of which drove across the causeway, around the cliff drive, ascending to the mesa upon which stood the Mosque of the sultan of Jahore, an imposing and solitary edifice. We were permitted to enter, after removing our shoes. The interior, however, disappointed us, characterized as it is by the musty air and appointments usual to a typical Midwestern court house.

On the return to Singapore, the two sections traded places, our section returning by train, while the other drove back in the automobiles. This railroad, by the way, is the main line between Singapore and Bangkok, a distance of eight hundred miles. The journey would represent a run of scarcely twenty-four hours

Around the World at Seventeen

in our country, but here, with swamps, jungles, and mountains to be traversed, it requires a week.

Again the two sections exchanged places, and we drove through huge rubber plantations for thirty miles, to a rubber factory, the nearness of which was heralded by atrocious fumes familiar to any one who has been in a vulcanizing plant.

Back to Singapore and lunch at the Thomas Cook Sweet Shop. One is surprised to find such peculiarly American dainties as iced cantaloupes, Post Toasties with cream, club sandwiches and other dishes familiar to us.

After lunch, we went to the Hotel Europa, where Killick, Robinson and Patterson decided to make certain additions to their wardrobes; so we telephoned a native tailor to come to the hotel to take their measurements for three pongee suits, monkey jackets, and "shorts." Until we reached Singapore, we did not encounter "shorts." They are an abbreviated trousers, worn with brogues and golf socks, leaving a section of the knee exposed. Nowhere in the world can clothing be had for less money. The boys picked three of the very best suits from the tailor's samples at the unheard-of price of six dollars each; these outfits were made up and delivered before the boat sailed the next day.

Most of the third day we spent at the Raffles Hotel. There are a number of hotels known the world over,

Around the World at Seventeen

such as the Moana, Honolulu; Imperial, Tokyo; Majestic, Shanghai; Raffles, Singapore; Taj Mahal, Bombay; Shepperd's, Cairo; Savoy and Cecil, London. The Raffles Hotel was the gathering place of the élite in Singapore. In the afternoon and evening every one sat on its broad verandas drinking iced tea and listening to the music of a very good band. These affairs are always colorful and one meets distinguished persons.

On the fourth day we spent a most interesting time in the police courts. This was due to Robinson's interest in legal proceedings. We watched a white-wigged, black-mantled judge sentence twenty-five or thirty petty thieves without even one glance at the culprits. There certainly is nothing cumbersome or slow about the Britisher's way of dishing up justice. In two hours, this judge decided more cases than a similar court in our country would decide in a month. We returned to the Thomas Cook Sweet Shop for lunch and remained there until we sailed for Batavia at six o'clock.

All night the *Ryndam* hovered near the Equator, but not until eleven o'clock the next morning, while we were at classes, did we hear the sharp blast of the ship's whistle, heralding the arrival of King Neptune and his court. For the majority of us, it was our first trip across the Equator. Of course, Captain Lieuwen, in forty years' sea faring, had crossed many

Around the World at Seventeen

times; but I think the prize goes to the ship's young wireless operator, a man not over thirty, with a record of seventeen crossings. Classes were dismissed and the boat given over for two hours to the sea god. To initiate all the novices on board was out of the question; therefore, representative members of the student body and the crew were chosen for the sacrifice. The selection was based on the victim's popularity, or lack of it, great bulk or lack of activity, general laziness and fastidiousness of dress. At least those prerequisites held with the student body; among the crew it was probably a case of first come first served. The women cruise members, of course, were exempt.

Before the last shrill blast of the whistle died away the entire ship, excepting only a few members of the engine crew, had gathered on the bridge and upper decks to watch the fun. Already, King Neptune occupied his flower-decked throne under a canopy of flags, at one end of the boat deck, not far from the swimming tank. Neptune was a huge stoker from whose broad, scowling face flowed a tawny, rope-hair beard that reached to his waist. On his head rested a crown of glittering, gold tinsel, and his huge, hairy paw gripped a scepter of the same glittering material. About him were grouped members of the crew dressed for the occasion like buccaneers and Malay pirates, while a few wore women's dresses. With their grotesquely painted faces, they presented a

Around the World at Seventeen

fierce looking ensemble. A chair was placed in an open space in front of King Neptune. One by one, the victims were led to this torture seat; their faces first were smeared with tar, then powdered with flour, after which a burly buccaneer, wielding an enormous razor, scraped the sticky mixture from the grimacing prisoner's face. Another servitor stood ready with a bucket of grease and paint brush, with which he finished up the job by smearing the unfortunate's face and hair thoroughly with the rancid liquid. Then the gasping novice was hurled into the tank of water, where he remained until twenty-five or thirty had shared a like fate. After two hours of this fun we were all given our Equatorial passports signed by King Neptune, himself; and then we adjourned to lunch.

The next day we reached Batavia, a port which the Dutch crew anticipated visiting, because many of them had relatives in Java. A word about the Dutch in Java before we reach Batavia, the capital. In Manila we saw an example of American colonization; in India we were to see a British protectorate. From all I could gather in our four day stay in Java, the Dutch surpass both Yankee and Englishman in successful colonization. As a matter of course, a brief stay of four days gave me scant opportunity to examine minutely the Dutch civilization encountered

Around the World at Seventeen

in Java. It is the smallest of the Great Sunda Isles, yet recent figures place the value of its exports at one and a half billion guilders per annum. A guilder is about forty cents in our money. Relatively one-fifth the size of Texas, Java, under Dutch rule, has developed its native resources to a greater extent than any like colony of any other nation in the world.

The *Ryndam* docked at Tandjong-Prick, where we disembarked to take a fast train to Batavia, ten miles distant. The railroad service was excellent, and in less than ten minutes after boarding the train we drew into the station at Batavia. Here a slight confusion occurred, no one apparently knowing just what to do next. Across from the station was a large market place, and following our noses, the five hundred cruisers meandered through the shops and down the street, until finally, we found the automobiles which were to convey us on a trip through the city.

Our first stop was at a Dutch church, three hundred years old, that commemorates the coming of the Hollanders to Java. Here we spent an hour, most of it awaiting the arrival of a priest who unlocked a huge padlock with a key that must have weighed four pounds. While waiting we were entertained by a flock of venders crying their wares at us. We next visited the Aquarium, which is not as good as the one at Honolulu. Our next stop was at a museum filled

Around the World at Seventeen

with relics from the temple of Borobudur. The temple, which I regretted my failure to see, is supposed to be the second finest in the world.

With our appetites sharpened by the ride, we repaired to the Hotel den Nederlanden for lunch. In the afternoon we resumed our sight-seeing with a drive through the streets of the capital. Batavia is a commercial city, modern and sanitary. It contains the steep gabled houses and walled canals of old Holland. Dutch names are everywhere in evidence, such as: Weltevreden, the principal quarter, and Buitenzorg, a suburb, famous for the Botanical Gardens, founded more than a century ago. Everywhere the quaintness of Holland has been blended with the exotic beauties of the tropics.

At four o'clock we were freed from further itineraries, and Patterson, Robinson and I went back to the Hotel den Nederlanden for a Dutch lunch. While we were enjoying our repast, Killick showed up with a most picturesque-looking Dutch character, whom he introduced as "The General."

The General reminded me of the Boer War pictures of the gnarled, massive, outstanding old Dutch generals of the Paul Kruger type, who caused the British army overtime work to subdue the Transvaal. On a head of flowing white hair rested a battered pith helmet; a broad face set with small gray eyes, a large bulbous nose, and generous mouth, surrounded by a

Around the World at Seventeen

bushy beard, emphasized the likeness to the old Boer veterans. Tightly held under his right arm was an odd-looking contraption, which I finally identified as a carburetor off an old car. What purpose it served and what part he served in the community, we were at a loss to determine. As Killick introduced each by name, we stood up, saluted, and gravely shook hands. Then we sat down and ordered drinks all around.

The General had a slight command of English but his conversation was mostly monosyllabic and certainly not brilliant. Meanwhile, we were sizing him up, as we invariably did any character we ran across, for possibilities in the way of entertainment or information.

After fifteen minutes thus spent, he turned suddenly to me and said, "Let's go!"

"Where to?" I asked.

He raised his hand impatiently, as if to strike me, and growled, "What do you care where we go?"

"All right, General," I said, "where you will."

"Get a taxi, then," he said.

We filed out to the street and piled into a taxicab, after which the General gave the driver directions in guttural Dutch, and we sped on our way, not knowing where we were going, or what lay ahead of us.

Finally we came to a suburb, and again the General growled an order to the driver. The car drew up to the curb and the old man got out, motioning us to remain seated; and he and his precious carburetor disappeared. By this time we were highly amused and kidded Killick over his gullibility. We figured the old man had finessed us for a free ride home.

But presently he returned, got in, and gave the driver more instructions. Our interest in him lay mainly in a desire to learn who he was, yet he so cunningly worded his replies that our rather pointed questions remained unsatisfied, while we could not grow angry with him. There he sat as substantial as the Town Hall, and as mysterious as the Flying Dutchman.

By this time we were at the edge of the suburb, and the taxicab drew up before an imposing edifice, the purpose of which we could not determine, and the General led us up the steps through a long lobby, lined on either side with offices in which a multitude of clerks were busy over typewriters, ledgers and file cases. Not having a great deal of confidence in our guide, we felt foolish at this intrusion upon such busy people. At sight of us, a gentleman came forward, to whom the General introduced us with great formality.

This man spoke good English, and politely expressed pleasure at meeting American students and trusted we would have a pleasant stay in Batavia. Then he hurried away before we got in a question

Around the World at Seventeen

edgewise. As a matter of fact, we never did learn what it was all about nor the nature of the place the General took us. After the man hurried away the General seemed satisfied that he had done his part and he led us back to the car, and back to the street where he had disposed of the carburetor, and there, without a word, he left us, and did not return. We waited for him awhile, feeling like snipe hunters holding the bag, then returned to the Hotel den Nederlanden for dinner. I have often wondered if the General was "touched in the head," as the Indians say, or was just an old bum who imposed on travelers. In either case, he furnished an adventure that made my stay in Batavia interesting.

Following an evening spent on shipboard watching a native dance performance, we arose too late to make the train to Bandoeng. Instead we spent the day in town. We found excellent Dutch lunches consisting of fresh baked fish, wiener schnitzels, and sauerkraut. During the day, Robinson, Killick and I experienced our first ride in the funny little two-wheeled cabs, something like the Irish jaunting carts. Two passengers sit beside the driver, looking forward, while two face rearward, the occupants bobbing up and down with every motion of the trotting horse.

A dance that night, given by the Globe-Trotters at the Hotel den Nederlanden, furnished excuse for an-

Around the World at Seventeen

other late sleep, and we missed a second trip, this time to Buitenzorg. I was not sorry to miss more sightseeing, however, as my eyes, due perhaps, to the constant sun glare in the tropical country, were becoming inflamed and swollen—so much so, in fact, that all the last day of our stay in Bangkok, I was forced to wear smoked glasses; and not until the boat sailed for Colombo, at five o'clock p.m., was I sufficiently recovered to again take interest in life.

CHAPTER EIGHTEEN

THE next point of interest on our cruise was our sailing over the submerged crater of Krakatao, which lies between Batavia and Colombo. At eleven o'clock the *Ryndam* hove to for the night, for the purpose of picking up our mail, which we had missed at Batavia. The real reason, however, for the delay was to permit a daylight passage over the great crater. Situated in the Strait of Sunda, between Java and Sumatra, the island remains of Krakatao belong to the Malay Archipelago. At one time this shattered group was a single large island rising from the sea to an elevation of 2,817 feet. Here occurred the most terrific explosion the world has ever known. On August 26, and 27, 1883, the volcano sent death and destruction to 36,000 people. Ships within a radius of two hundred miles were covered with soot and lava dust; and following the eruption three days of darkness, caused by the clouds of smoke and lava, settled over the land. The *Ryndam's* course lay directly over the crater, passing between the jagged edges that once were the apex of Krakatao. In the sunlight, the rocky cliffs of these islands presented colors of a thousand hues, their sides seared with great

Around the World at Seventeen

perpendicular channels, down which coursed the molten lava during those fateful two days.

The passage from Batavia to Colombo covered seven days, the longest unbroken voyage since leaving Honolulu. We recrossed the Equator December 23, with Christmas Day only two days off.

It rained all day the 24th; a play was given that night, but every one's thoughts were of home. Altogether, Christmas Eve was not without its sentiment. But Christmas Day! Despite every one's attempt to "pep up" for the occasion, a general spirit of gloom settled over the boat. We had missed our Christmas mail at Batavia, and what is Christmas without presents! In addition, it was my first holidays spent away from home. A few students received radiograms, but to most of us the day was like the others, unbroken in the monotony of tropical heat. Some writers say no one has enjoyed a perfect Christmas until they have spent it on the ocean. That may hold good with people of artistic temperament, but I prefer to spend mine at home. We really had a wonderful Christmas dinner, and a series of entertainments later. A carnival was held, stalls erected, where home-made candies and little knickknacks were auctioned off, the proceeds going into a pot for the benefit of the ship's crew.

One more day at sea, with a temperature hovering around 110 degrees, and we anchored in the bay off

Around the World at Seventeen

Colombo. The heat was at baking point when we took tenders for the dock. I do not exaggerate when I say that Colombo was hard on the eyes. The little Singhalese city radiates irresistible charm and color, but the houses are dazzling in their whiteness, with the earth very red and the skies deepest blue. It is this combination that affects one's eyes.

At the dock, autos awaited us and we rode down the main street of Colombo, with not a soul in sight, despite the midday hour. The town has only two main streets, paralleling each other, a white clock tower sentineling one of these. We turned at this tower and rode down a narrow street to the Cinnamon Gardens, where we saw trees from which comes the sweet fragrant bark familiar in every household. Hawkers, here, sold strings of beads and necklaces made of the little brown cinnamon berries, the scent of which seems to be imperishable.

We later visited the old churches and forts reminiscent of Portuguese and Dutch occupation, and the ancient native Pettah quarters, known to the English as Black Town. This section teems with every variety of race and costume. The Singhalese, although the blackest race we had yet encountered, are good looking people, with classic features.

During the morning drive, we visited the Buddhist temple, Kelaniya, after removing our shoes as usual. The approach to the shrine was up a flight of stairs

Around the World at Seventeen

through an imposing gateway. Arriving at the upper terrace, we found natives kneeling before the walled-off Bo Tree shrine. On our return to the town, Killick, Patterson, Robinson and I lunched at the Galle Face Hotel. Several incidents marred the pleasure of the occasion. For one thing, the food was poor, and the prices outrageously high, thirty-two rupees, an equivalent of eleven dollars for the four. Also in getting money exchanged at the desk we were charged almost double the regular rate of exchange. But what displeased me most, although it caused the others to laugh, was that I was not permitted to smoke my pipe in the dining-room. In fact, the waiter was insolent, snatching the pipe from my mouth with the gruff remark, "You can't smoke your pipe in here, sir!" To which I replied, "Then I'll get out!" And I did, followed by the laughter of the other three.

In agreeable contrast to our experience at the Galle Face, a trip made to Mount Lavinia Grand Hotel forms a pleasant recollection. We hired rickshas for the mile drive around a wonderful beach, fringed with ferns on the one hand, and lapped by the bluest expanse of ocean imaginable. Apropos of rickshas, it is timely to remark that Colombo was the first port for some time where I have mentioned them. Neither Manila nor Batavia had these handy man-drawn vehicles, due, I learned, to the laziness of the coolie class

Around the World at Seventeen

in both Java and the Philippines. But here on the ocean drive, sheltered from the rays of the sun by a widespread umbrella, we once again enjoyed the jiggling motion of the pleasant little carriages.

We approached Mount Lavinia Grand Hotel over a narrow causeway reminiscent of the moat and drawbridge of a medieval castle. Charm is perhaps the single word that best describes this hostelry. Not until we were seated on the terrace overlooking the ocean did we feel the need of superlatives. The hotel itself is old-fashioned but very complete in appointments. It is built on a knoll that rises two hundred feet above the beach, with sheer cliffs facing the water. More beautiful, I think, than Waikiki, the beach sands are swept by gentle breakers and are the bather's paradise. In silhouette against the limitless expanse of ocean blue, graceful drooping palms nod gently in the breeze. Seated under the umbrella on the terrace, sipping a cold beverage, one gives himself up to relaxation, while all about him, like the bustle of lazy bees, comes the hum of subdued conversation.

We rode back to Colombo over the same wonderful beach road, through clusters of native settlements. Everywhere in the Orient, we were besieged by beggars. Colombo, unfortunately, was no exception. The means these creatures use to mutilate themselves in order to get pity from the travelers is both amazing and repulsive. One grows callous to the sight of

Around the World at Seventeen

them and is filled with anger rather than pity. There are cases where a beggar has kept his arms folded across his breast until the arms have withered and have grown together. A more common form of mutilation is to force an iron bar through a cheek or the bridge of the nose, and even drive a round pebble into the center of the forehead until the flesh about it holds the stone in place.

At the downtown hotel, the beggars swarmed about us chattering and offering their amber wares for our inspection. Amber seems to be the stock-in-trade of the Oriental beggar. Irritated beyond measure at their tactics, we had them test the genuineness of the amber by fire. I am sure the dirty crew burned up several pounds of their stock before we threw them a handful of *annas* and dismissed them, their mutterings of anger and disappointment sounding in our ears until they disappeared from sight.

We dined, spent the evening and night on the *Ryndam* in preparation for an early start to Kanday, whither we were to go by special train. If one's time is limited in Ceylon, by all means pass up Colombo and go to Kanday. The railroad journey back and forth alone is worth while. Our train consisted of an ample number of compartment coaches, similar to those we later encountered on the continent. Killick, Robinson, Patterson and I had a section to ourselves, but this was one train trip where we did not

Around the World at Seventeen

indulge in bridge to pass the time. The scenery reminded me of the Georgetown Loop and other beautiful vistas in our Rocky Mountains. Up a torturous grade, at the speed of a fast mail packet, we whirled past cocoanut groves, alternating with jungles of wildest grandeur. Hugging the brow of deep-cut gorges, we passed through one winding tunnel after another, by sparkling waterfalls, and over summits whose beauty reminded me of the hills of New England.

Absorbed in the endless magnificence of the scenery, we arrived only too quickly at Kanday. This fortified town was the former capital of Ceylon, where resided the Kanday kings, famous in story and legend. The trip to the ancient capital is supposed to be the most beautiful in the world. Kanday is clean, charming and picturesque. Autos met us at the station and conveyed us to the Botanical Gardens where every shrub and plant is labeled for the convenience of the visitor. Next we visited the Temple of the Tooth where the former Kanday kings worshiped. We were still in the land of Buddhism, and there inside the dark and gloomy temple we found the usual big statue of the god.

We next visited the Sacred Elephants, not so sacred, however, but that the priests could forget their religion long enough to charge two rupees for the curious visitor to mount them. We had an excellent meal

Around the World at Seventeen

at the Queen's Hotel and took the train back to Colombo and the boat.

Before leaving Manila, Mr. Carson Taylor gave me a card of introduction to a Mr. Barlow, of the Sun Life Insurance Company. Killick and I found Mr. Barlow, an immaculately dressed gentleman, at his desk, and on our presenting Mr. Taylor's card, he asked how he could serve us. The question was a poser. We had looked to him to take the initiative and perhaps suggest something out of the ordinary. In previous chance meetings, my luck had held. For a moment Mr. Barlow studied the situation with knitted brows.

"I'll tell you what," he finally said, "I am not using my car and chauffeur just now. Suppose you take them for a little drive. Return later and lunch with me at the club."

We thanked him for his kindness, and in a few moments we were seated in a Rolls Royce limousine, a spick-and-span chauffeur at the wheel, headed for Mount Lavinia Grand Hotel.

We chose that destination for several reasons. We knew the cruise, full force, was at the hotel. Driving up in a Rolls Royce, with a uniformed chauffeur, would create a satisfying impression—satisfying to us; furthermore, we longed to sit once more on the terrace and gaze upon the restful scene. All of which, in due course, came about. Afterward, we

Around the World at Seventeen

rode away with great éclat, and returned to Mr. Barlow's office where we picked him up and proceeded to the Colombo club to an excellent lunch.

The year of our Lord, 1926, passed out the second day at sea, and New Year's Day was ushered in on a wave of unprecedented heat. In spite of the weather, however, every one was excited over the prospect of the Taj Mahal trip, the most important event in the extensive itinerary planned for our stay at Bombay. New Year's Day went off rather cheerfully, culminating in a real banquet and later in a creditable vaudeville performance given by student players. Not once since leaving Colombo were we out of sight of the low-hanging, palm-fringed mainland, with the breezeless ocean lying like glass and the nagging heat enveloping the ship. Three days of this and we sighted Bombay, the last port before the *Ryndam* turned its nose toward Cairo, and home.

CHAPTER NINETEEN

"The Gateway to India!" The cradle of mysticism, occultism, symbolism! We anchored three miles off shore early in the morning. Before us spread the shoreline of Bombay with its ten miles of water front, its population of more than a million. From the boat, the city presented a front as substantial as John Bull himself. There was nothing of India in sight, but behind that solid array of modern European buildings, in byways and highways, we knew that interesting people, with strange customs, were packed.

After lunch, tenders drew alongside the *Ryndam* to take us ashore. The most important building seen from our landing place was the Taj Mahal Hotel. Standing at the water's edge, with something of the significance of our own Statue of Liberty, towers the monumental Gateway through which all must pass who set foot upon India. It is a twenty-minute ride from the boat to the base of the steps at the Apollo Bunder, where one disembarks to pass through the magnificent marble arch of the Gateway.

After lunching at the Taj Mahal Hotel, the most pretentious hostelry in all India, we went for an extended drive through the business section of the city. The size of Bombay impresses one, such a huge jumble

Around the World at Seventeen

of peoples held in leash, one might say, by the cold justice of the temperate Englishman. Wherever conditions necessitate modern utilities to facilitate efficiency, British appliances are used. Typical London double-deck omnibuses lumber along the streets; tram cars, likewise double-decked, add to the British atmosphere. Tobacco stores, haberdashers, book stalls—indeed, here one finds a dozen Piccadillys. Spice this strongly Anglophile atmosphere with defiant-looking Hindu priests in vivid yellow gowns, beggars squatting at every turn, and the native snake charmers, and you will have a good first impression of India as seen in Bombay. To me the symbol of India was the snake charmer's fife, with its weird, haunting, tuneless melody. Not once during our six days' stay in the country did I see an ugly snake charmer.

We beheld two interesting although rather gruesome spectacles. The first of these was the Hindu burial grounds where we witnessed the native method of cremating the remains of the departed. We passed through a gateway in a high stone wall and saw what seemed to be a cord of wood piled up. Near by was a still form on a stretcher surrounded by a crowd of natives, wailing and chanting hymns. A native touched a match to the woodpile and a flame leaped up. Thereupon the bearers raised the body from the stretcher and laid it on the funeral pyre. This spectacle was too much for many of the cruise and they turned away unable to stomach the sight.

But even more interesting was the burial of the Parsees. Bombay is famous for these fire worshipers, who follow the religion of the ancient Persians. Mostly prosperous merchants, they number about fifty thousand. To reach the burial ground we made a steep climb up to the top of a hill where stand the so-called "Towers of Silence," five in number, each possibly one hundred feet high. On top of them the dead are laid in troughs, and left there exposed to the elements and the vultures until the bones are picked clean. These troughs radiate from a common center in the circular towers, with a drain-pipe so the rainfall will wash the refuse to the ground below and scatter it in the dust under the feet of passers-by. The Parsees dispose of the dead in this manner in order that the dust of high caste and low may mingle in common, symbolizing a return of all souls to an equal plane. We, of course, did not see the tops of these towers, but a plan describing them is inclosed in a glass case where the visitors to the beautiful adjoining grounds may gain an understanding of this form of burial.

We reëntered the cars and from the Towers of Silence were driven up another long hill which terminates in a mountain ridge, or hogback, where we stopped for a wonderful two-sided view. Many hun-

Around the World at Seventeen

dred feet below us, on our right, sprawled Bombay, with an aeroplane view of the Gateway and beyond it the *Ryndam* riding at anchor. Turning from this scene of human congestion, we looked leftward down upon a low rolling country, dotted here and there with beautiful estates surrounded by gardens.

While yet we were thus engaged, I heard weird notes and saw a little way ahead of us, squatting in the middle of the road, with two large wicker hampers beside him, a snake charmer swaying in unison with the high, liquid notes he wooed from a fife. This instrument with which the snake charmer lures the spectator, as well as pacifies his cobras, bears a resemblance to his venomous pets. A bagpipe effect a short way from the mouthpiece dilates and contracts much in the manner the cobra dilates its neck into a broad hood; only there is a deal of difference between the melody thus wrung from the fife and the terrifying hiss emitted by an angry cobra.

When the snake charmer struck up his weird strains, seventy or more of the cruise gathered around him and he lost no time in "passing the hat," or rather a turban, in exchange for contributions offering us entertainment in the way of a fight between a cobra and a mongoos. Nearly every one knows what a cobra looks like, the most unsightly as well as the most deadly of all snakes; but the mongoos, perhaps, is not quite so familiar. He has a head like a squirrel's and

Around the World at Seventeen

a body somewhat like a beaver's, short forelegs and slender body increasing in size toward a tail similar to a mountain rat's. The mongoos' chief weapon is its razor-like teeth.

The snake charmer, a handsome Hindu, was not satisfied with our first offering and he bickered with our crowd for "more rupees or no fight." He spoke English perfectly, as do all Indiamen whose varied callings bring them in contact with the Anglo-Saxon.

After the snake charmer fussed and cajoled for a while, meantime making a pretense of returning his pets to their hamper prisons, some members of the cruise added a few rupees to the contribution and the fight was on. In India, a mongoos-cobra fight is a sporting event of importance similar to the cockfight in Spanish settlements. The cobra rears its head in the air, with hood dilated and emitting an angry hissing, and strikes at the dodging, darting mongoos in an attempt to deal death with its poisonous fangs. The mongoos' play is to attack the snake in such a manner that its sharp teeth will close over the varmint's head, thus rendering useless the cobra's needle-like weapons. After obtaining such a hold, the mongoos quickly crushes to death the helpless cobra. The fight begins when the snake charmer runs his naked hand into a hamper and brings forth a wriggling, hissing cobra which makes no attempt to strike its master's hand; then, after placing the snake in the

Around the World at Seventeen

cleared circle, he reaches into the second basket and hauls forth a shrieking mongoos on leash. The cobra and the mongoos are instinctive enemies and there is no time lost in preliminaries. In the manner above described we saw a mongoos kill two cobras, but not until the little animal himself wobbled from weariness and the repeated bites of the varmint.

Then the snake charmer called for more rupees to stage a fight between an eight-foot non-poisonous snake and the mongoos. Again the rupees were forthcoming, but we protested when the huge reptile slowly began twining its deadly coils about the almost helpless and quite dazed mongoos. Responding to the protests, the snake charmer brought forth a fresh mongoos which managed to bite the big snake until it was in a state of stupor and the combatants were separated. The mongoos was declared the winner by popular vote.

It was now lunch time and my crowd, consisting of Killick, Patterson and myself, returned to the Apollo Bunder. A more leisurely inspection of the Gateway arouses in the mind of the observer an admiration for the British. One senses in its architecture, its square-shouldered, rugged solidity, the qualities in the Englishman which have made him pre-eminently an empire builder. The Gateway was constructed in 1917, to commemorate the reign of King George and Queen Mary, and symbolizes the growth

Around the World at Seventeen

of an Empire upon which, somewhere on the globe, the sun is always shining.

With half the world put behind us, we considered ourselves seasoned travelers, and what now happened proves the old adage, "Pride goeth before a fall." Also, it proves that a traveler must ever be on guard against certain nimble-witted gentry of foreign lands. On leaving the *Ryndam,* our attention was called immediately to the imposing Taj Mahal Hotel only a few steps from the Gateway. For some reason we temporarily forgot its whereabouts and hailed a taxicab, ordering the driver to take us to the hotel. Instead of pointing to the hotel and saying, "There it is, gentlemen," he bundled us in his car and drove through the streets a roundabout way and back again to the hotel. Of course, we saw how we had been "gypped," but there was nothing to do but pay and go our way.

The Taj Mahal Hotel is one of the most notable hotels in the world—and, I might say, the most expensive in proportion to the services rendered. In name, reminiscent of the Taj Mahal, which later we were to travel a thousand miles to see, it holds a glamour for the traveler. We found it truly wonderful, with its softly lighted, richly tapestried balconies overlooking the spacious lobby, with its excellent band, which played "God Save the King," while every one stood at attention, and its elaborate dinners.

Around the World at Seventeen

We returned to the *Ryndam* for the night, and the next morning, early, tenders arrived to convey us to the Elephanta Caves, on an island about half an hour's sail from the boat. The approach to the island is so shallow that we were transferred from the tenders to rowboats, and from them we walked up flight after flight of stone steps to the top of a mountain. Here we found huge grottos hewn out of the rocks with the roofs in many places supported by stone columns, uniformly carved, resembling somewhat the columnar work of the ancient Phœnicians. In these grottos we found relics a thousand years old and older; pictures carved on the walls illustrated various precepts of Hindu philosophy. These pictures, by the way, are thousands of years old, mute evidence of the antiquity of Indian civilization. An educated Hindu lectured to us for two hours on the significance of these pictographs, making all the more interesting our visit. Among other things of interest was a great stone elephant in a tropical dell near the grottos, carved by unknown hands, from which the caves derived their names.

In the afternoon we returned to the *Ryndam* to pack for our trip to Agra. Paul Robinson was in the sick bay and had not accompanied us on our recent excursions. Cecil Champitt replaced him in our group of four. After our preparations for Agra we still had a little time on our hands so we taxied out

Around the World at Seventeen

to the seacoast to a quaint Italian resort where we were ushered upstairs into a private dining-room. In a billiard room adjoining, we whiled away the time before we partook of an excellent Italian dinner.

At 5:25 o'clock we left the Victoria Station for Agra, with the long-looked-for Taj Mahal as our objective. Before us lay a journey requiring three nights and two days, the round trip covering a distance of practically two thousand miles, merely to obtain a transitory view of a single *objet d'arts*—and not a very comfortable ride at that.

Our discomfort, however, was not due to the lack of train facilities. With true British thoroughness, the Government railroad furnished us an excellent train of compartment carriages. My group occupied a compartment to itself. Before we left, the cruise management warned us to lay in a supply of water, as that on the carriages was not suitable for drinking purposes. Otherwise our compartment was all to be desired, quite commodious, with ample lounging seats and double-deck berths, and a private bath. We solved the question of drinks in various ways, in the main preferring the juice from the East Indian tangerine, the most delicious and thirst-quenching fruit in the world. We laid in a bushel supply of this first cousin to the orange; at our journey's end a corner of our compartment was heaped high with yellow peelings.

Around the World at Seventeen

In many respects, the thousand-mile, night-and-day, one-way journey across the very heart of India was the most remarkable I have ever taken. We were a carefree bunch, filled with pleasant anticipation of the treat in store for us, and we used devious and ingenious ways to pass the time. We "kidded" the persistent and impudent beggars who whined at every window and door when the train stopped at the stations, and were highly amused at the mendicants' blaspheming. Their retorts, I am quite sure, would have laid us low, if Allah had been lacking in mercy. Fortunately, both windows and doors of our compartment were inclosed in a darkish glass, which while it permitted us a clear view of the outside world prevented our being seen. Another form of amusement was trying to bathe with our carriage in motion. Rolling as we did like a ship in a storm-tossed sea, the process furnished more sport than my surf-board ride at Waikiki.

In lieu of a Pullman porter we had a native bearer, a man who spoke fluent Cockney. "Stud," as we called him, was obtuse and slow to grasp the point of our crude American jokes. How very applicable is the word "pun" when applied to a Britisher's effort at humor! In the suggestion of those two words, pun and joke, lies the difference between Americans and our British cousins. Stud, along with his Cockney lingo, had acquired the British inability to grasp quickly our Americanisms. But he stood for our horse-play, knowing, as do all foreigners, the lavish tip the American usually dispenses.

While the dust literally fogged about us when the train was in motion, the weather was pleasantly cool; quite a contrast to the temperature we were forced to endure on board the *Ryndam* before arriving at Bombay. Excellent meals were served at the way-stations, and thoroughly enjoyed, if one were lucky enough to be in the forefront of the rush of disembarking the moment the train slowed down. Accordingly, sometimes we ate, and at other times we ate—tangerines. This sounds like an English pun, but really was of serious moment, although we did not object to tangerines.

Despite the cool weather and the seeming mildness of the sun's rays we were warned against the danger of sun-stroke. At one of the way-stations where we were to dine, in my mad rush to gain a table, I forgot my hat, but an official made me return for it—insuring safety to my head at a cost to my stomach.

In this wise, at an early morning hour we arrived at Agra, and began the most eventful day of the two hundred-odd spent on the world cruise.

CHAPTER TWENTY

OUR itinerary in Agra included two special points of interest—the Fort of Agra and Taj Mahal. More, perhaps, than any other city in India, Agra, due to its constantly imperiled position, is dear to lovers of romance and adventure. The country through which we passed to reach the ancient capital is similar in topography to that of our native Indiana. There is a gradual rise from sea level to an elevation of nearly a thousand feet, to the foot-hills of the highest of all mountain ranges, the Himalayas. We found here in the dead of winter a most salubrious climate, although our palm beach suits were certainly out of season.

As I want my readers to get the most possible out of my trip to Agra, I will attempt to give the historical and geographical background of the ancient capital. Situated in a great rolling plateau, and watered by the deltas of both the Ganges and Jumna rivers, this city of two hundred thousand inhabitants was the frontier defense of the Aryan stock against their Western neighbors, the hereditary free-booters occupying the highlands of Central India. Geographically, no place was better situated for both a trading center and a strategic base for an extensive army. Jehangir relates in his autobiography that be-

Around the World at Seventeen

fore his father, Akbar, built the present fort, the town was defended by a citadel of great antiquity. For three hundred years, it had been the habit of the Afghans and the other wild tribes to descend from the higher plateaus of the Northlands and found kingdoms, with their power radiating from Belhi and Agra. It was Sikandar, of the house of Lodi, A. D. 1500, the last of the Afghan dynasties, who grasped the strategic importance of Agra to enable him to keep in check his rebellious vassals to the south. Sikandar thereon moved his court to Agra, which, from being a "mere village of old standing," became the most important capital in India. But it remained for the Emperor Baber to capture the city in 1526, the famous Koh-i-noor diamond being part of the loot. He announced his invasion was a permanent conquest and not a temporary occupation. Akbar, the builder of the present fort, was the conqueror's grandson.

On our arrival at the Agra station, desiring to avoid the crowd, we quickly got into one of the two-wheeled carts and departed for the Fort. The carts, by the way, resembled the Irish jaunting ones, drawn by a native pony, with room beside the driver for one passenger, the others facing the rear. We galloped through the gravel streets of the picturesque old town and by eight o'clock arrived at the Fort.

Due to its dimensions one can see the Fort only piecemeal. Its strong and lofty walls of red sand-

THE TAJ MAHAL

Around the World at Seventeen

stone are a mile and a half in circumference. It is my impression that I was told the Fort was never taken by force. Not an improbable statement for the bastioned minareted walls lend the impression of a strength more formidable than Gibraltar's.

For three hours we explored the Fort from turret to catacombs. I had an "up in the air" feeling as I stood on the topmost walls and gazed out across the city. Situated on a bluff of the Jumna River, the Fort commands a great scope of country. While promenading along the top of the thick-set, sand-stone walls I gained my first view of the Taj Mahal, with its domes and minarets glistening like a white jewel in the morning sunlight.

From this elevation we descended to the level of the immense court yard in the parade ground. Patterson and Killick were with me, and securing a guide we next essayed a trip through the catacombs. We were led through a narrow door, and down musty, worn stone steps which descend abruptly into a large chamber. Every one groped his way by the aid of a candle. The guide warned us to be on the lookout for snakes. In fact, the catacombs are so infested by reptiles that many of the passageways are sealed. The guide told us that one of these led all the way to Delhi, a distance of approximately two hundred miles; through another, a man rode horseback to the Taj Mahal.

Returning to the surface, we visited a number of

famous buildings of the Fort. Two of these represent the finest example of pure Hindu architecture—the red stone palace of Shah Jahan, the builder of Taj Mahal; and the Moti Masjid, or Pearl Mosque.

The latter we visited first, and to our relief were not compelled to remove our shoes. The exterior of the mosque is of pure white marble, surmounted by three large circular domes, flanked by six smaller towers all of the same material and workmanship. On entering the cool recesses of the edifice, we found ourselves in the prayerchamber, the marble floor of which was laid out in squares, every one of a size large enough to accommodate a kneeling Mohammedan. These squares face a large archway paneled with precious wood, which frames a niche representing Mecca, the seat of Mohammedanism, toward which the prayers of the Faithful are directed.

The palace and pavilion of Shah Jahan is more interesting still, with its background of romance and legend. It, too, is of white marble inlaid with precious stones. The sides of the palace facing the court yard form a right angle, with a cool corridor running the full length. At the end of the right wing a small bridgeway extends, with marble floor. In the center of its snowy whiteness is embedded a great slab of black marble. The story goes that in a siege, a hot cannonade was directed against the palace, but one shot only struck the roof of the right wing, the

Around the World at Seventeen

heavy ball bounded off to the bridgeway adjoining, and struck the black marble slab. No damage resulted, but later a great stain of blood appeared on the spot where the cannon ball struck the black marble. The palace is of particular interest because here lived Shah Jahan, the builder of what is said to be the most splendidly poetical building in the world. One can see the domes of the Taj from the balcony which juts out in a circular form from the main wall of the Fort. On this overhanging gallery Jahan spent his last hours gazing upon the mausoleum of his departed wife—Muntaz Mahal. In the white marble wall of the pavilion is a series of large perforations, like lacquered lattice work; the inner wall is of black marble, and, whether by intention or by accident, the miniature image of the Taj Mahal is reflected thereon.

We spent more time at the Fort than we anticipated; already the crowd of students had overtaken us. In order to again assume the lead we three, Patterson, Killick and I reëntered our jaunting cart and instructed the driver to make haste to the Taj Mahal. This he did, and we raced through parkways lined with perfect trees. At a sudden turn we came upon a breath-taking view of the mausoleum.

I have already stated that the Taj Mahal is the most splendidly poetical building in the world. Indeed, words cannot adequately describe it; yet, I will do my poor best. The Taj, begun in the year A. D. 1632,

Around the World at Seventeen

represents thirty years of patient, skilled work. It was built by the Emperor Shah Jahan as the last resting place of his favorite wife, Muntaz Mahal; and he himself lies buried at her side. The Taj was designed by Ustad Isa, who was either a Byzantine Turk or a native Persian of Shiraz—probably the latter, as the marble work undoubtedly belongs to the Persian school of workmanship. The noble structure can be described as a dream in marble. There is a saying that the Moguls designed like Titians and finished like jewelers. In purely decorative workmanship, in the perfect symmetry of its exterior, in the aerial grace of its domes, rising like marble bubbles into the azure sky, the Taj knows no peer. Lord Roberts, in his *Forty Years in India,* says to those who have not beheld it, "Go to India. The Taj alone is well worth the journey,"—a statement which in my opinion, is not exaggerated. Neither the passage of time nor the erosion of weather have marred the fresh beauty of Taj Mahal. It is said that after the noble pile was completed, Shah Jahan blinded the craftsmen lest they might attempt to duplicate the architecture.

An imposing gateway, scarcely less beautiful than the mausoleum, guards the entrance to the grounds. Here we gazed at the reflected image of the Taj in a marble-rimmed pond extending from our feet to the steps of the main structure. A score of fountains placed at regular intervals in the pond added their showers of scintillating water to the brilliant scene,

Around the World at Seventeen

and symmetrical trees contrasted their deep green with the marble whiteness.

In fact, the landscape gardening of the grounds was no less beautiful and striking than the mausoleum itself. The grounds and buildings are under British government supervision, which, of course, accounts for their continual state of preservation.

The main building is of marble, chaste in its whiteness, crowned with four great domes. From the corners of the marble terrace which surrounds it, rise domed minarets of like material. Two beautiful temples, likewise of white marble, flank the Taj.

Without a guide or the usual candles, we climbed the dark spiral stairways of each of the four minarets; and from the little pavilions above we gained different views of the main structure. In the clear sunlight it appeared dazzling white, blinding the eyes. Then we turned to the Taj proper, and climbing a flight of marble steps to a platform fully a hundred feet deep, passed under a great archway into the building. I placed my hand on the marble wall; it was cold as ice.

We then entered the main chamber to gaze at the tombs, side by side, which inclosed the remains of the lovers. The Taj is so finely proportioned that it suggests nothing of the spectacular. Indeed, the judgment displayed in style and ornament and proportions conveys a high idea of the taste and skill of the architects of the age. The tombs are screened off but easily accessible. In this chamber the inlay and carving are exquisite. Indeed, every spandrel of the Taj, all the angles and more important architectural details, are enriched with the inlay of such precious stones as agates, bloodstones, jasper, and onyx. Striking in color, they are combined in wreaths, scrolls, and frets, and form the most beautiful and precious style of ornament ever adopted in architecture.

After dining at a pleasant hotel, Killick and I returned to the Taj to see it for the last time and by moonlight. The quiet of the evening, the ghost-white buildings that seemed to float in the air above the dark foreground of shrubbery, the charm of the historic and romantic background, enthralls one, and we lingered as long as we dared, departing with regret for the train that was to leave for Bombay at nine o'clock.

Our return journey was similar to the one bringing us to Agra. All night, all day, another night of travel, and we arrived at Bombay at five in the morning, in time to board the tenders at the Apollo Bunder and cross the rippling bay at sunrise. We breakfasted on board the *Ryndam* and returned once again to the city where we stocked up with provisions for the five day trip to Aden. We had our last look at Bombay and the Gate of India in the gathering dusk as the *Ryndam* steamed slowly out of the bay.

CHAPTER TWENTY-ONE

THE five days at sea were hopeful ones. With only one port of call, Aden, between us and Cairo, we would soon be in European waters. Saturday, January 8, was the 113th day—the halfway point of the cruise. For a time we sailed southward toward the Equator, with the weather growing cooler. When we again turned northward it grew correspondingly hot. Studies were resumed, and for five days the usual shipboard routine was maintained.

Aden was not disappointing because we expected little. The colony is non-productive. The town of Aden lies in what is probably the crater of an extinct volcano and is surrounded by precipitous rocks. The British Government subsidizes the Arab chiefs, and the city, with the Island of Perim, at the entrance of the Red Sea, is under the jurisdiction of the Bombay government. All food is imported and the water supply is chiefly obtained from condensation of salt water and from an aqueduct seven miles long, built in 1867. Aden is a very old town, having once been captured by the Romans about 24 B. C., and by the Turks in 1538. The Arabs regained control in the following century and in 1837, after the maltreatment of the crew and passengers of a wrecked British

Around the World at Seventeen

vessel, the British Government took possession and annexed the territory to India.

We spent one day only at Aden; enough, considering what we found there. The town is built around a crescent, hedged in by the hills. Beyond lies the great, arid Arabian desert similar to the Arizona wastes. We missed the tropical verdure, the cooling breezes of tree-lined parkways. The people, in the main, wore fezes and went barefooted. They were not particularly clean. Beggars and hawkers heckled us at every turn, fawning upon us to buy their ostrich feathers and fans of poor grade, and blaspheming when we refused to be inveigled. Due to a disease quite prevalent in Aden, many of the men have only one eye, which gives them a malevolent appearance.

In the afternoon a fleet of Ford busses driven by wild one-eyed drivers, conveyed us up a hill to Maala, where we embarked in a train of coaches equipped with log seats, and were driven across the desert over a bumpy track twenty-five miles to Lahej. Here lives the Sultan in a pretentious palace surrounded by squat, plastered adobe buildings, the whole inclosed with a high wall. We were permitted to peer at these habitats and their denizens through the pickets of a tall fence. These barbarians were anything but handsome and conveyed an impression of their mean dispositions by the curved scimitars and pistols which they wore in their belts.

WITH THE SULTAN OF LAHEJ—ARABIA

Around the World at Seventeen

Lahej is in a little oasis where the blinding glare of the desert is relieved by small groves of huge date palms. In some unaccountable manner the natives had acquired a stock of American fifty cent pieces which they graciously sold us for ten cents a coin, their own money. Killick managed to pick up quite a supply. On the other hand, I bought three dollars of the Arabic money, of which I spent not a cent, and returned it for a dollar-seventy. The robbers!

We stayed long enough for a group of fifty, including our professors, to gain an audience with His Highness the Sultan of Lahej; then we returned to Aden and sailed for Suez.

Next morning we passed out of the Gulf of Aden, through the Strait of Dad-el-Manded, and from there into the Red Sea. I think the most desolate object I have ever beheld was a lighthouse, ninety-five miles from Aden where the keeper lives with his children, year in and out.

Despite the terrific heat, the traveler is supposed to encounter in the Red Sea, we found the weather bracing and pleasant. At the time, we did not realize that we had put behind us the heat of the tropics. For the next three days we sailed between the mountain-rimmed coastlines of Arabia and Africa, until finally we came to Suez, at the entrance of the famous canal. Theoretically we entered the canal two miles out from Suez. Port Said lies at the Mediterranean end.

Around the World at Seventeen

The canal is 88 miles long, 25 miles being through the Bitter Lakes. Ferdinand de Lesseps, who later failed at Panama, was the French engineer who began its construction in 1859; ten years later it was opened for trade.

We remained no longer at Suez than necessary to board the train for Cairo, a distance of 80 miles; and on the journey, through dust and sand, we passed many little Egyptian stations and saw tall Egytian soldiers marching in squads and singly across the desert. As we approached the Nile Valley, the country took on the aspect of Catarina, in the Winter Garden section of Texas. Here we passed clean little towns with walls of snowy whiteness, and mosques with white minarets. No sight was queerer, however, than that of a Lipton Tea sign in one of these desert villages. In time we passed through suburbs not unlike those of Chicago, and came to a stop in the commodious Cairo railroad station.

On stepping from the train, we were greeted with a medley of sounds that struck on our ears like the *honk-honk* of flying geese. It was the first intimation we had had of our nearness to Europe. Hitherto, we were greeted with the brittle sounding klaxons of American made cars. In Cairo we saw our first fleet of French and Italian machines. All European cars are equipped with large nickel-plated and brass horns, such as the American makers abandoned years

Around the World at Seventeen

ago; and these drivers toot their horns at every opportunity. In the main, the cars we now entered were the last word in luxury and we sank back into the soft cushions as we were whisked through Parisian boulevards, past modern continental buildings and substantial stone barracks garrisoned by Egyptian soldiers.

Our destination was the Heliopolis Palace Hotel, which is situated in one of the beautiful suburbs of Cairo, twenty minutes from the downtown section. Cairo reminds one of Paris, in every respect being a metropolitan city, the only difference to the casual eye being the fez worn by the men. Everybody wears them, although in Egypt this form of headdress is called the tarboosh. Later I went to a tarbooshery, had my head measured, and saw them steam and stretch this form of skull cap to fit me.

The Heliopolis Palace Hotel was built to rival the Casino at Monte Carlo. In architecture, surroundings, and appointments, it succeeded in its purpose; but it failed to lure the gambling bloods from their old haunts and was converted into a hotel. As such it catered to a luxury-loving public. The palace extends for two blocks, surrounded by commodious and artistic gardens and grounds. It is in the district of Heliopolis, a suburb made beautiful by houses of modern Spanish architecture. At an easily accessible distance are coffee shops, hair-dressing parlors, gro-

Around the World at Seventeen

cery and delicatessen shops, billiard rooms, and flower shops. There is a choice of dining either in the hotel or in one of the little French or Italian restaurants set in cozy nooks surrounded by palm trees.

We were the first guests of the season and were met in the entrance by an army of newly uniformed porters whose dress reminded me of Valentino in *The Sheik*. Patterson, Killick, and I were assigned an enormous room, with three beds, a fireplace but no heat. Overhead hung a great crystal chandelier and the floor was carpeted with the finest of Persian rugs.

After an excellent dinner in the enormous ball room we wandered out into the lobby, seeking as usual for the unusual. Standing alone was a tall, handsome man, dressed in the uniform of the Egyptian cavalry. He looked interesting, and we sauntered casually past him a time or two before he noticed us. When he did, he came forward and introduced himself as Captain Kadr, a Turkish officer of the Egyptian Cavalry, and asked us how we would like to see the Nile by moonlight. Needless to say, Killick and I accepted the invitation and with the captain driving a new sedan, and two companions whom he introduced as his nephews, we rode through the downtown section, past the Municipal Theater and scores of open-air cafés, where the crowds seated at dinner in formal evening dress reminded one very much of Paris. We found Captain Kadr both inter-

Around the World at Seventeen

esting and informative, and congratulated ourselves on meeting him.

At Cairo, the Nile is about the size of the Missouri River at Kansas City, and in the bright moonlight it looked like a silvery flood. An island in the river forms one of the exclusive residential districts, and is connected to the mainland by a long, well-lighted bridge. It was not a particularly wide bridge, nor was it a desirable point for a tire to blow out, which was our luck midway across the structure. But no further mishap occurred, and we saw the famous river by the light of the desert moon, and returned safely to the Heliopolis, where we bade Captain Kadr good night after making an early-hour appointment to see his Arabian pony perform.

The next morning at nine o'clock the captain called for us and Killick and I walked up a hill with him to an old baronial castle. Again Patterson refused to join us, and he missed a treat. While we stood on the sloping lawn, the captain led out a wonderful cream-colored Arabian stallion which he immediately mounted and put through his paces. Not only was the horse intelligent, but he had the speed of the wind. A turn of the knee guided him; the gesture of a hand brought him from breakneck speed to a full stop. He had all the tricks of the circus-trained horse, and the grace of his movements excelled anything I had ever witnessed in horseflesh.

Around the World at Seventeen

The weather was delightful. As we stood there watching the captain and his stallion, a crowd of cruise members, who were visiting the old castle above us, turned to watch the horseman, no doubt wondering what part we played in the exhibition.

We returned to the hotel for lunch and prepared for an afternoon group trip to the native section. Patterson rejoined me, but Killick chased off somewhere looking for an interview with some famous personage—his usual stunt in every port.

On these group trips one gained a general idea of people and customs, but due to the rapidity with which we moved from point to point no intensive study could be made. My general impression of Egypt might be summed up in the statement that we are the youth of races; they, the grandparents. I had the same feeling I often had when looking into the face of an Indian in our West; the light of ages lies in the misty darkness of their eyes. The buildings of the native section are not unlike those of a Mexican border town—the walls of plastered adobe, trellised windows, and flat roofs. An occasional veiled woman appeared at a window, and on the roofs people foregathered in the evening as they do in Mexican patios.

We wound in and out of the labyrinth of streets and finally emerged high on a hill above Cairo at the gate of the Mosque of Mahomet Ali. This edifice

Around the World at Seventeen

was generally spoken of as the Mosque of Two Thousand Lights. Here a commanding view was had of the Nile and the desert with two pyramids in the distance. As invariable in Mohammedan mosques, a niche before which the faithful pray indicates the direction of Mecca. The main chamber of the mosque is circular with an enormous dome, the whole decorated with scrolls, friezes, and paintings of high artistic merit. Suspended from the dome are the two thousand lights, the crystal prisms of the chandeliers reflecting the colors of the rainbow. On one side of the niche, a spiral stairway leads to an overhead station where the priest intones his sermon. There are many legends extant which thrill the credulous traveler. On one of the pillars supporting the great dome, seven feet from the base, is the well-defined print of a horse's hoof. In ancient times, we were told, the mosque was the scene of a battle where the dead lay piled six feet deep. Over this human mass rode the conquerors and a horse left the imprint of his foot on the pillar. On another pillar is the imprint of a bloody hand. Again, some say they see Christ's image as He hung on the Cross, an effect produced by the sun at a certain angle. It is my personal opinion that the priests keep the blood stains freshened and dig the imprint of the horse's hoof a little deeper, all for the benefit of the tourists.

CHAPTER TWENTY-TWO

WE next visited the mosque of Sultan Hassan and the Egyptian Museum, which was of great interest at the moment as King Tut's treasures were on exhibit. The time passed until we were due to arrive at Groppi's Tea Room, where we were to assemble at the invitation of the Egyptian students.

Groppi's is one of the world's outstanding places of refreshment. With a seating capacity of three or four thousand, it easily accommodated the cruise members and our hosts, the Egyptian students from the various native universities. A tea is a much more elaborate function in the East than with us. Groppi's is famous for its caterers and chefs, and specializes in fine *pasteles* and Egyptian dishes, as well as excellent tea. The guests are served at tables in a wonderfully scented garden an acre in extent and canopied with an awning.

Patterson and I had the good fortune to meet two Egyptian law students, Issa Abd El Hay Moustapha and Ahmed Abu Bakr, who vied with each other in showing us a good time. They were perfect hosts. Indeed, on the whole cruise, nowhere did we find such good fellowship and general intelligence. They

Around the World at Seventeen

spoke English perfectly. When I say perfectly, I mean with Websterian precision—not as we Americans speak it.

Imagine our surprise when one of them confided to us that never before had he *spoken* our language; that we were the first Americans with whom he had had the pleasure to converse! Yet the statement need not be an exaggeration. The Egyptian impressed me as being the product of so many ages of intellectual development, of such a rich heritage of scientific achievement, that he learns most readily. Indeed, while we knew precious little of their country and history, these students knew every detail of ours. The scope of their information was truly amazing. Hence, before we left Cairo, I accepted without question the Egyptian's statement that he had never before spoken English.

For the next half hour we had a highly interesting and amusing time. The Egyptian student body was in ordinary evening dress, but all wore the tarboosh, or fez. This headpiece is similar to that worn by the Shriners; and we amused ourselves by politely inquiring what was their lodge, and asking other inane questions.

Suddenly, a great shout came from the main doorway. We turned and saw a lone Egyptian standing with his hands outstretched. The hum of conversation and the tinkle of tea-cups ceased instantly. The

Around the World at Seventeen

next moment with one accord the assembly arose and a mighty shout rocked the tea room, "Long live Zaghlul Pash!" This was repeated three times; then everybody sat down. Behind the crier came a dignified, elderly man, whom we learned was the Speaker of the House of Representatives. The crier preceded him to a table where the dignitary sat down. Then another shout arose, and again everybody stood up, in response to—"Long live America!" This cry likewise was repeated three times before seats were resumed. Zaghlul Pash then arose and in a well-worded speech, in English, welcomed the American students. He was followed by the American Ambassador who evoked a laugh from the Egyptians present by stating that he did not know whether he was Egyptian or American. Dean Lough, on behalf of the Floating University, responded, and then the table talk was resumed. After tea, our two Egyptian friends took us back to the Heliopolis in their car.

We dined at the Heliopolis, after which Mustopha and Bakr returned for Patterson and me, having invited us to their home to drink coffee and listen to Egyptian music. After a ride of some length, we drew up to an iron trellised gate before which paced a sheiky-looking person whom Mustopha addressed as "Amed." The sheik was the valet of the family, and he opened the gate, bowing low at a further order from Mustopha to prepare coffee. We entered the house, which resembled a French chalet. The room

Around the World at Seventeen

into which our friends conducted us corresponds to the drawing-room of a luxuriously furnished home. Here, while we awaited the coffee, Mustopha put an Egyptian record on his Victrola. We were glad when the coffee arrived. Egyptian coffee is served in tiny cups and is about half liquid, half dregs. You are supposed to drink the former and eat the latter. Patterson, in retaliation for my encouraging the Egyptian music, consumed three cups with much gusto, forcing me to appear equally enthusiastic. My eye, in wandering about the room, lit on a peculiar-looking musical instrument occupying the place of honor among several others. This instrument, which had nine strings and was gourd shaped, was inlaid with mother-of-pearl and wonderful stones. I wondered what sort of music it would produce and asked Mustopha to play it. Apologizing beforehand for his poor ability, he took it down, and never have I heard an instrument give forth such harmonies as this one did under his magic touch. Even Patterson enjoyed it.

But a still greater treat was in store for us. Our friends suggested we drive across the Nile and see the Pyramids by moonlight. There was a good paved road all the way, and a street car line, both ending at the Mina House Hotel, built to accommodate the hosts of tourists. The hotel is a hundred yards from the foot of Cheops, and the pavement terminates in a concrete parking-place for automobiles. Electric

Around the World at Seventeen

signs are everywhere. Strange to say, no photographer has ever dared to desecrate the popular conception of the Pyramids' remoteness on the desert by showing how civilization has encroached on their solitude. For the benefit of the sentimental, guides conduct parties out a mile or so to supposedly lonely desert camps. The tourist must indeed have a vivid imagination to lose sight of the electric signs displayed on the tall buildings of Cairo.

When we parked the car, I stepped out on the opposite side from the others, and when I looked around, they had disappeared. There was nothing for me to do but climb back in the car and wait their reappearance. Which I did for two hours. Not knowing the extent of our itinerary when we left the Heliopolis, neither Patterson nor I had brought overcoats; and there I sat shivering, with a raw night wind blowing and the water, which, wherever it formed into pools, was frozen over.

Sitting there in the car I could hear the night sounds, not of the desert, as one might suppose, but the shouts of one tourist friend to another, in this wise—"Watch your step, Jim! That darned rock is loose!" and again—"Jerusalem! Ain't there no top to the darned thing—how fur is it, Bill, up there?" These and sundry other Americanisms transported me from the Nile country to our own free-spoken and breezy West. America certainly was abroad on this night despite the freezing weather.

Around the World at Seventeen

When Patterson and the Egyptians returned they were surprised to find me waiting, thinking all along that I had gone on an excursion of my own. Patterson had climbed almost to the top of Cheops. He, too, was almost frozen, and Mustopha and Bakr suggested that we go to the Mina House Hotel to warm up. There was a ball in progress and we were politely and pointedly turned away as neither Patterson nor I were wearing dress-suits. But we were told if we would slip around the back way we could get hot coffee.

We spent the next morning at the Heliopolis, resting from the previous day's exertion and trying to keep warm. In the afternoon, however, things brightened up. We went to the University of Egypt to witness the defeat of our soccer team, 3 to 2. The Egyptians gave the greatest exhibition of soccer I ever saw. A short time before the native boys had decisively defeated the champions of England, the home of soccer football. After the first half of the game, it was plain that our boys were far outmatched. Whereupon, the two teams were divided, each one about equally Americans and Egyptians; then the game became interesting. Howard Marshall, the star goal guard from Haverford College, was the only American player who really knew the game; and his playing was brilliant. Zaghlul Pash and many other Egyptian officials were present, and all remarked on

Around the World at Seventeen

Marshall's outstanding performance. After tea at the university, we returned to Heliopolis for the night.

As might be deduced, I saw little of the Pyramids by moonlight. The day following the soccer game, the cruise made a group trip to the same point. Patterson, claiming a business engagement, refused to go. Anyhow, he probably discovered the night he climbed Cheops that he was not missing much.

The charm of the Pyramids was lost on me. In the first place, the bold play made for the traveler's money, the petty grafting of the guides and dragomen, filled me with disgust. Perhaps, also, my not being an enthusiastic Egyptologist nor especially interested in ruins and monuments relating to the early history of the human race, had much to do with my indifference. However, I did pretty much the usual thing: rode a lumbering camel to the Sphinx and climbed Cheops, the oldest of the Pyramids. The Sphinx looked her age and in accordance with present day fashion, she was getting her face lifted. Workmen on scaffolding could be seen chiseling and sweeping and patching up her wrinkles. In "doing" the Pyramids, I made the climb in my overcoat and was worn out when I reached the top. I reached the top in forty-five minutes, after seven stops, about the average climbing speed. In photographs, the Pyramids appear to come to a sharp apex; in reality their tops are twenty feet square. I was told that the

Around the World at Seventeen

erosion of the weather has decreased their height by twenty feet and their width thirty-five.

While resting on the top, a native boy, of perhaps twelve, came up to me and offered to wager five dollars he could descend Cheops, run to the nearest pyramid, climb it, descend and return to me, all in eight minutes by my watch. Incredulous though I was, I did not bite. Later I learned that he not only could make the round trip in the time stated, but if the disgruntled better was not satisfied, he would make a second and even a third trip, each time clipping thirty seconds from his schedule. This boy knew every step and stone and had his speed so well timed that he could gauge accurately his progress. The baby movie stars had nothing on him as a bread winner for his family.

In almost every port the shrewd natives had figured out some such graft. When I climbed the four dark, spiral stairways of the minarets at Taj Mahal, I encountered another youthful grafter. Arriving at the top of the stairway, while overlooking the Taj, I heard a rustling noise below. In the darkness I descried a young beggar who offered to light my way down the steep stair. I waved him away; but he refused to be waved, and as I descended he struck an endless number of matches, which despite my wish served to light me safely down. Of course, I tipped him. It became a game between us, and despite my efforts to shake him, he succeeded in repeating the service on

Around the World at Seventeen

three of the four stairways. Another gentle graft is to be taken to the Nile to see the bulrushes where Moses was found by the Queen. After showing me the spot, the insinuating dragoman whispered in my ear that for the price of another *piaster* he would show me the starting point of Moses' watery journey. The joke lies in the fact that in Moses' time the Nile, a constantly shifting river, was several hundred yards away from its present channel, and the wiley dragomen instead of showing us Moses' bulrushes really was giving a performance of "rushing the bull."

Getting back to Ghizen and the Pyramids, we spent the forenoon taking in the sights, and returned to the Heliopolis for lunch. The afternoon was taken up by another itinerary through Cairo, visiting museums and the El Ezbekiyed Gardens, about which centers the modern life of the city. Sunshine and color meet the eye at every turn. Beyond question, Cairo was delightful, surrounded as we were by the luxury of a cosmopolitan city, midst a people both friendly and ready to dispense hospitality.

It was with real regret we bade our Egyptian friends, Mustopha and Bakr, as well as the comforts of the Heliopolis, good-by and boarded the train for Port Said, where the *Ryndam* awaited us. I stayed on the boat, as did the majority of the cruise members; therefore, I saw nothing of Port Said, the northern entrance to the Suez Canal. At five p.m., we sailed for Haifa, and the Holy Land.

CHAPTER TWENTY-THREE

HAIFA lies at the foot of Mount Carmel, and is the best natural harbor on the Palestine coast. The site is that of classic Sycaminum, but the present town is entirely modern, its development dating from 1890. We paused here long enough to take an early train for Jerusalem.

After a five hour ride through a hilly, rocky country, we arrived at the largest and most interesting city in the Holy Land. Were I a Bible student, or twenty years older, I might have been more appreciative of the things we saw in the Holy Land. With out any desire to be irreverent, I have the impression that much we saw was fake. I will do the best I can to separate the wheat from the chaff, however, and let the sensible reader draw his own conclusions. In the first place, the Holy Land is not for travelers who are unversed in Biblical history. Serious students might be willing to put up with poor hotels, the lack of heating or lighting plants, few baths, poor food, and where much of the sightseeing must be done on foot, as automobiles can not find passage inside the walled city.

We were met at the station, outside the walls, by a fleet of cars, and were driven to Bethlehem. There are no forests in the Holy Land, and Bethlehem sprawls over a rocky, sandy hillside. We were first driven to the Church of Nativity and descended to the Manger room where Christ was born. I use the word descended because since the time of Christ the town has filled in until it is thirty-five feet higher than of old. The Manger room is draped in cheap tapestries, with a few old paintings on the walls, and lighted candles are placed around the spot once occupied by the manger.

The weather was unbearably cold, and after a brief shivering stay at Bethlehem, we returned to Jerusalem. We next went to the Mount of Olives, where we viewed the tower from which Christ made the Holy Ascension. This tower was disappointingly new in appearance, but from it we viewed the River Jordan and the Sea of Galilee. No growing plants or crops were anywhere seen. We returned to the city, where Patterson and I put up at the Casanova Monastery, while the remainder of the cruise were housed in hotels outside the wall.

We arose early the next morning and in groups started on "foot-back" to see Jerusalem. We first visited the Holy Sepulcher, and found it to be a cold, damp place filled with Christmas-tree decorations and wax candles. At the Station of the Cross, one decoration which might have been beautiful—a great swinging chandelier—was swathed in heavy cloth. We

Around the World at Seventeen

next walked along the Via Dolorosa, stopping to hear a brief lecture on what had occurred there at each of the seven stations where Christ stopped. These stations led up narrow, winding cobble-stone steps with overhead archways at intervals, by means of which the inhabitants passed from one building to another.

In the afternoon we went to David's tomb at the Jews' Wailing Wall. Since our visit, the wall has been condemned, but when we were there the wailing was in full swing. A number of old men read the Bible so constantly that religious fervor overcame them. When their emotions reached flood tide and their tears flowed down their cheeks, they would rest their heads upon an arm against the wall and weep aloud.

Later, Patterson and I strolled along the Via Dolorosa at midday and we saw a few more intimate details of native life—donkeys packed with loaves of bread; meat carried in the same manner followed by swarms of flies; dirty children and dirty streets; no automobiles, carts, or wagons; steps which we went up and down; an occasional leper, and beggars everywhere—that, to me, is Jerusalem. At five o'clock from the towers in all parts of the city Mohammedan priests call the Faithful to prayer. Fezes are everywhere in evidence emblematic of the Mussulman. Christians were scarce—and this is the birthplace of Christianity!

Perhaps the most interesting and authentic place

Around the World at Seventeen

we visited was the King Solomon Temple area. We passed through a gateway into the extensive grounds of these ruins and beheld first, the Dome of the Rock, an octagonal shaped building, surmounted by a huge dome. This structure apparently serves only to preserve a great rock, under which extend King Solomon's Quarries, where one can walk a great distance underground. Near the reputed site of Solomon's palace, also underground, were the stables where it is said he kept 2,000 horses.

We spent another night at the Casanova Monastery and were awakened by a monk at six o'clock to prepare for our trip to Nazareth. Unfortunately we chose a car without a top and suffered accordingly from the extreme cold. The country through which we drove was mountainous and very beautiful. Jacob's field and well were pointed out to us. Arriving at Nazareth we lunched at another Casanova Monastery and went to the Virgin Mary's house, peered into the cistern known as Mary's Well, and visited the carpenter shop of Joseph, where Jesus worked for twelve years. There was nothing of particular interest to me between Nazareth and Haifa, which port we reached in time to sail at eight o'clock for Constantinople.

On the first afternoon of the four days' voyage, we passed the Isle of Cyprus, the view of snow-capped Mount Olympus forming a pleasing relief after our

Around the World at Seventeen

long stay in the tropics. The next day we passed many islands noted for their mythical legends, while a hundred miles away on the mainland towered more snow-capped mountains. Early morning of the last day before docking at Constantinople, found us entering the Dardanelles, with the squat town of Chanak opposite. Despite the coldness of the weather, I obtained a seat of vantage on the prow of the boat while we sailed through the famous Straits.

On Monday, January 31, we docked for the first time since Batavia. Constantinople, with a population of 1,200,000 is divided into four sections, Pera, Galata, Stamboul, and Scutari. As seen from the New Bridge in the Galata section, the Turkish capital reminds one of San Francisco. Here also, we encountered, for the first time since leaving Los Angeles, the European mode of dress. Most of us have always associated the Terrible Turk with the fez, but a law has been enacted prohibiting the native headdress, and the fedora, cap, and top-hat are worn everywhere.

On disembarking from the boat, we were driven through the busy downtown streets directly to the Mosque of Sultan Achmed, commonly known as the Blue Mosque. Patterson, Killick and I were assigned a woman guide who clucked at us like an old hen with a brood of chickens. Seasoned travelers that we were, we showed our displeasure at her officious man-

Around the World at Seventeen

ner by trying to shake her at every opportunity.

Our next stop was at the Mosque of St. Sophia, recognized as one of the Seven Wonders of the World. The dome of this great mosque is a hundred feet across, with a tall minaret guarding each of the four corners of the structure. In my opinion the Blue Mosque is far more beautiful. Once again on entering these edifices, we were compelled to remove our shoes, but the carpeted floors of the Blue Mosque were less cold than the bare stone we trod in St. Sophia.

We left the mosques to enter a sort of pool-room, with steps leading underground from a dark rear corner. By means of these we entered the Basilica Cisterns, a subterranean water-way extending for miles, upheld by concrete pillars, and electrically lighted. Boats, in which one could ride for hours, plied back and forth on the water, through various well-lighted chambers. While the cisterns are now very shallow, we were told that at one time they were thirty-five feet deep.

We were next taken for a drive through the streets and residential section—a drive that furnished ample thrills, for beyond question, Constantinople has the wildest taxi drivers in the world. A closer view of the city bore out my first impression that it resembles San Francisco, although it is several times larger. After an hour thus spent we were driven to the Turkish University, passing through an enormous gateway

Around the World at Seventeen

much more imposing than the University buildings we later visited. Here we had tea and attended a reception given by the native students, and later visited a number of museums where we saw in action the last of the Whirling Dervishes. The Turkish Government long since suppressed these religious fanatics but keeps a group of them at the museum to illustrate their barbarous practices. These fanatics staged an exhibition for us, whirling and shouting to the monotonous beat of tom-toms.

But the queerest and most interesting sights we saw in the museums were the wax images. The Turks excel in wax work. You pass down the long corridors lined with these images, conscious that eyes are boring through your back. You turn, startled. What at first seems to be a human being proves to be a wax image, very life-like, with amazingly human eyes. These figures are placed in all sorts of positions; here two are in the posture of shaking hands; there, a group surrounds a speaker, listening attentively to his oration; family groups; harem scenes; armored knights; and merchants displaying their wares. In this manner, Turkish life is illustrated in a manner both interesting and instructive.

After two hours spent in this museum, we returned to the boat for the night. The next day we were free from group trips, so Patterson and I started out early for a walk through the city. One point of interest we visited was the Galata Bridge. Here a toll of one *piestre* per person, is exacted. It is estimated that 400,000 people cross the bridge every day. We then visited the *American Express,* the largest daily newspaper in Constantinople, and later trudged up the long hill to the top of Pera. But try as we would, the city is so large and scattered we never got beyond the business section. The streets were the busiest I ever saw, and the cold, bracing air gave us energy. From the hills in Pera we had a splendid bird's-eye view of the city.

After a two hours' hike, we went to Robert College, where we witnessed a basketball game between the college and the Turkish University. We later had tea and returned to the boat to sail at six o'clock for Greece.

On the whole I liked Constantinople, in every sense a cosmopolitan city. The Greek influence predominates, although the Armenians lead as merchants. The Armenians, in fact, wherever I saw their stores or homes, impressed me as being a wealthy class; far from the conception we have at home, where Armenian Relief Funds to relieve the poor, struggling race are solicited everywhere.

We arrived at Piræus and were driven in comfortable cars over a two-way paved road to Athens. The history of Piræus is practically that of Athens, to which it has been the sea port since Themistocles

Around the World at Seventeen

urged the Athenians to take advantage of the natural harbor, instead of the sandy bay of Phaleron. The harbor city probably dates from the time of Pericles. It was destroyed by the Romans in 86 B. C. and until a hundred years ago was only a fishing village known as Porto Leone. The ancient name, Piræus, was revived by independent Greece in 1833. Since that time it has grown in population to 300,000. It is a town of factories. Wines and cognac are produced in quantities for export.

Present day Athens looks not unlike a prosperous American city, with its buildings and hotels of modern architecture and wide streets with tramways. The persistent beggar is not nearly so noticeable here as in the Orient, but there are hundreds of post-card venders. The modern innovations detract from the ruins of ancient times; nor can one expect in a brief two days to make more than a cursory inspection of the crumbling, history-laden piles. Greece and Palestine were the only two ports of call where I essayed no side trips, but was content to make the conventional cruise trips.

Arriving at Athens, we drove immediately to Mars Hill, and the Acropolis, the crowning glory of old Greece. The approach to the Acropolis is over a wide, winding gravel road, bordered with plants not unlike the blue-green bladed maguey of the Spanish Southwest. The buildings of the classic citadel are

Around the World at Seventeen

not as large as I had been led to believe from photographs. Perhaps its unimpressiveness is due to its location, for one's attention is constantly drawn to the magnificent view of all Athens and a great sweep of country extending to the snow-capped mountains toward Corinth.

One grows mute in the presence of these symbols of departed greatness. Shades of the Immortals! Demosthenes, Pericles, and Sophocles trod these same stones which we, the student travelers, now trod. The stately pillars, pregnant with meaning, towered in silent greatness above a square-shouldered, fortlike foundation. On approaching the East front one is impressed with the strategic location of the citadel, the Hill of the War God—Mars. How well named; and yet when one reaches the pillared ruins above thoughts of war fade away in the presence of the time-worn reminders of ancient Greece, leader of all times in sculpture, architecture, and philosophy.

We next visited the ruins of the Roman Theater just under Mars Hill. The vast amphitheater reminded us that Greece had her gladiators and athletes. Here we sat in a row of stone chairs, as lasting as time, and listened to Dean Howes lecture on ancient Greece.

The Parthenon, the Temple of the Wingless Victory, the Temple of Nike, the Temple of Jupiter, the Arch of Hadrian, and the Choragic Monument of

Around the World at Seventeen

Lysicrates, were each in turn visited. Words can not describe them, and photographs fall far short in the attempt to convey the beauty and significance of these classic remains. At the Parthenon the various Greek letter fraternities assembled in groups for their photographs. What would have been the ancient Greek's sensations if, standing under the massive columns of Theseus, they should have beheld a fleet of automobiles glide almost noiselessly up to the entrance of the temple! And yet these ancients supplied the world with our present day conceptions of the arts and sciences.

A basket lunch was sent from the *Ryndam,* which we ate in the Exhibition Hall of the Near East Relief building. Greek dancers entertained us during the repast, after which we drove to the new Stadium, a huge modern replacement of the ancient amphitheater where present day athletes hold their tournaments.

The weather, like love, is a subject of perpetual interest. One of the most interesting and best preserved buildings of ancient Greece is the Tower of Winds. This was the early Greeks' weather bureau; here they measured the rainfall, determined the direction of the prevailing wind, and kept the solons advised when to carry their umbrellas and overcoats. Intricate symbols are carved in stone and the walls are carved with weather prophecies.

Around the World at Seventeen

Greece is not for the casual traveler. One must be well versed in Grecian history; must know the meaning of every stone and every carved pillar to comprehend her great ruins. Dean Howes' lecture, illustrated by lantern slides, one night prior to landing at Piræus, prepared us on short notice to make the most of our visit to the ruins. To appreciate them one should not use our modern standards for comparison; one must really unlearn what the average man necessarily knows to survive the dangers and pitfalls of life to-day. Strip us of the knowledge of this commercial age and how little would we know in comparison to the ancients, of philosophy and of arts! The modern Greek is not so handsome as his forefathers; he lacks the refinement and perhaps the nobility that went with the greatest thinkers of all times. To us in America, they are known as cooks, rather than as statesmen.

CHAPTER TWENTY-FOUR

LEAVING Greece, we sailed for Ragusa, variously called Gravosa, or Bubrovnik, one of the chief ports of the present day Kingdom of the Serbs, Croats, and Slovenes. From the moment I looked out of the porthole, as Captain Lieuwen docked the *Ryndam* in the snug natural harbor of Ragusa, I liked the place. Ragusa by the Adriatic—another "Graustark" of fiction fame. Picturesque, romantic, restful to the eye. Here, I should like to spend days instead of the few hours allotted us.

Since leaving New York, with the single exception of our brief stop in Los Angeles, we had been among dark-skinned races. Now as we strolled along King Peter's Street the flaxen-haired, blue-eyed, rosy-cheeked men and women we met were pleasing to our eyes. The military was much in evidence, the officers in modish uniforms, heavily braided, and with medals decorating their breasts. Ragusa is a well fortified town. We followed a stairway that led us to the walls of the city, from whence we looked down on the craggy coast line of the Adriatic which was washing the rocks two hundred feet below us. The sea was calm as glass and as blue as indigo. On a huge crag that jutted from the mainland the massive walls

Around the World at Seventeen

of Fort Lorenzo loomed white against the blue background of sea and sky. Looking down into the town, the scene was no less picturesque, the tile roofs of the houses made colorful by the green, blue, and violet tile.

We strolled through the street of wonderful shops, with plate-glass windows in which the displays were as enticing as I later found in the shops of Paris. In the market place I loitered to feed the tame pigeons, and I drank from the cool, sparkling fountain under the shadow of Porte Pile. I passed through a gateway, dark as a dungeon keep, into the Dominican Cloister and stood by the well from which the monks drew their water supply.

Later I climbed the hill overlooking Ragusa, up a broad tree-lined avenue to the fine hotels near the top. It was the off season but I was informed that these hotels in the summer are frequented by royalty and fashionable society from Belgrade and Budapest. The gay life there accounts for Ragusa's being called the Balkan Riviera. I returned to the town below and had an excellent lunch at the Balkan Café, where flaxen-haired waitresses in the picturesque Serbian garb attended my wants. I stayed the time limit and had to hurry to make the boat, which sailed at five o'clock for Venice.

The entrance to the harbor of Venice is through the Malamecco canal at the lower extremity of a long

Around the World at Seventeen

offshore bar. When we entered the harbor at six in the morning a cold wind was blowing and a haze obscured a clear view of the Italian shore. I stood on deck shivering but eagerly anticipating my first glimpse of Venice—the City of Dreams. Gradually through the lifting haze loomed the buildings of the water front, with the tall tower we know as the Campanile breaking the otherwise even skyline. Venice, the far-famed Queen of the Adriatic, immortalized by Byron, the center of art, the most unique city on the earth—Venice, the incomparable!

The city rises on mud flats that form an island in a lagoon between the mainland and the long bar. On such an unsubstantial foundation is the imperishable city built. Its streets are mainly canals, and its churches and palaces are built on piles. Everywhere these foundations are constantly settling, as attested by the unevenness of floors and piazzas; Venice, indeed, struggles constantly to keep her head above the water. Because of its location off the mainland, Venice came into existence as the home of refugees who sought protection there from the raiding hordes of the Northland. As early as 466 A. D., it took on the dignity of a small state. The first Doge was elected in 1679 A. D. The city increased in power, expanded its territory to the mainland, until in 1380 it became absolute mistress of the Mediterranean and Levant trade. With the capture of Con-

Around the World at Seventeen

stantinople by the Turks, the first blow was dealt at Venetian supremacy. In 1797, Napoleon conquered the city and made it a vassal to Austria; but in 1866, it was united to the kingdom of Italy, and so remains a part to-day.

As we approached the Doge's Palace, before which we were to drop anchor, boats of every description flitted about us—speed boats filled with Venetian students, waving their handkerchiefs and beckoning us to join them. These boys were immaculately dressed in natty green capes thrown over their shoulders and jaunty caps surmounted with feathers, reminding me of Robin Hood's men minus their bows. Gondolas, too, were everywhere, in the main black in color, with their helmsmen standing erect in the stern, plying their long paddles with a churning stroke.

We were eager to disembark. But the doctors came aboard for ship's inspection, and to our consternation the boat was put in quarantine. Three members of the *Ryndam's* crew suffered a disease carried by the rat flea. Rumors were afloat that we would be held for thirty days and there was talk of abandoning the remainder of the cruise and sailing for New York. All day we remained in suspense; but finally at night, after every cruise member had undergone a rigid medical inspection, we were free to go ashore. This we did, six in each gondola.

With canals for streets, the city's unique transpor-

Around the World at Seventeen

tation system consists of "street car" motor boats and gondola water taxicabs. The former ply up and down the canals, having regular routes and making regular stops at important points, rendering the service of a metropolitan street railway system.

But the most important item of transportation in Venice is the gondola, its importance being comparable to the ricksha of the Orient. These swan-like boats first came into use in 1094, and during the days of Venetian supremacy were gayly painted and covered with rich embroideries. Due to a plague which almost wiped out the population, the city council passed an edict requiring all gondolas to be painted black, and the custom holds to this day.

There is also another type of boat much used, comparable to the town car of the much hurried business man. This is the sedan speed boat; and in early morning hours the Venetian man of affairs may be seen behind his wheel speeding jauntily down the streets of water to his office.

Venice is connected with the mainland by a railroad bridge 3,600 meters long. The Venice terminal station marks one end of the grand canal. In spite of its lack of solid streets, the city has a surprisingly efficient system of transportation. Hospitals have speed boat ambulances; the post-office has fast mail boats; the fire department is efficiently equipped with high powered crafts—but Venice has no horses, and

Around the World at Seventeen

but one automobile, the latter a little Fiat coupé proudly occupying a place in the show window of a back street. Here is a city where many of the younger generation have never seen a horse in the flesh. To make up for this, however, the horseless city possesses the best known and most remarkable equestrian statues in the world. The noblest of these stands in the Piazzo of San Marco hospital, in memory of the Italian general, Bartolommeo Colleoni. It was designed by Verrocchio. He worked on it for nine years but died before it was cast. It was unveiled in 1496. The church of Santos Giovanni Paole—the Pantheon of Venice—has four remarkable equestrian statues high against the wall over the tombs of noted generals. Classed amongst the noblest of modern statues are those of Garibaldi and King Victor Emanuel II. Four bronze horses, presumably the work of the Greek sculptor Lysippus, about the time of Alexander the Great, occupy a place on the façade of the Basilica of San Marco. They have been called The Four "Horses" of the Apocalypse. They were cast in gilt bronze but now their golden skins are covered with the autographs of tourists. These animals are a much traveled quartet. Whether they belonged originally at Athens is a question, but they once presided at the entrance of the Colosseum at Rome, with Victory as their driver; later, in the great Hippo-

Around the World at Seventeen

drome in Constantinople, where they were captured by the blind Doge Dondolas, in 1193, transported to Venice and placed in the center arch of San Marco. There they remained until they were captured by Napoleon in 1797, and taken to Paris. On the fall of the empire in 1815, a return of spoils brought them back to Venice.

Patterson, Robinson, Killick, and I started immediately for the Hotel Royal Danieli to eat a late dinner. The trip to the hotel in the gondola gave us our first glimpse of Venice by night. Colored lights everywhere cast their reflections on the rippling water; speed boats, luxurious in appointments, flitted past us; here and there a gay party made their way down to the landing every home having a quay of its own.

Thus entertained, we made our way to the Royal Danieli, paid our gondolier, and entered the brilliantly lighted, spacious lobby. A glimpse of the dining room and my heart sank; all Venice seemed to be dining there, and it was a laughing, happy Venice. The music from a first rate string band made a pleasant background for the hum of voices. Surely, something unusual was happening. We had about given up hope of getting a table when the *maître d'hôtel* himself came foward and led us to a far corner of the room where several waiters rushed forward to

Around the World at Seventeen

assist him in seating us at a table. We ordered ham omelets and were waiting the arrival of the food when a loud noise sounded in the lobby.

It developed that a group of university students heralded their coming by song. Venice is a university town; here the student body, not always studious, has the freedom of the place. American undergraduates, in a playful mood, can create considerable disturbance, but they have nothing on the group of six Venetian blades who now burst into the dining room with swank and swagger. They were dressed in brilliantly colored costumes and Napoleonic hats of red and yellow, covered with clinking medals. The color of their hats indicated the collegiate class to which they belonged; the medals were those won at track and field events. Our first impression was that they were celebrating some memorable victory, but later we learned they were on a money-raising expedition in behalf of their particular college. On meeting them we found them to be an intellectually eager group, in the main in age much beyond the average of our under-graduates. After dinner we strolled under the colonnade around the square and back to St. Mark's, to the water front, returning by gondola to the boat and to bed.

The next morning was free, and I went window shopping. The shops near St. Mark's Square, which is the artistic center of Venice, are both wonderful

Around the World at Seventeen

and expensive, famed for their fine leather goods and Venetian glassware. I found lower-priced shops farther away, with goods of similar quality, if my eyes did not deceive me. Patterson, Killick and I lunched together at the Olympia Restaurant, where they change the color of the linen three times a day; but the privilege of being served in this world-famed restaurant was hardly worth the nine dollars we paid for three plates!

Carrying out a program of retrenchment, after an afternoon spent strolling up and down the narrow sidewalks bordering the canals, watching the freight boats with their cumbersome burdens, the black gondolas, and the flashy speed boats, we dined at Luna's on spaghetti, and saw Robinson off on the train to meet his mother in Naples.

Time hung heavily with Killick and me after Robinson's departure. We three had been almost constant companions on our various expeditions. We wandered into a movie theater, where we saw our first picture in five months. Afterward, we sought a coffee shop, where we had coffee, not so much from the need of the drink as to watch the complicated machinery our order set in motion. The Italian, like all Latins, likes his coffee second only perhaps to *Cinzano,* a grape cordial.

Our third and last day in Venice proved the most interesting. As every one knows, Venice is famous for the manufacture of exquisite glassware. We saw the blowers at work, dexterously shaping beautifully symmetrical articles from ungainly lumps of red hot glass. Furthermore, the trip by street car boat to and from these factories gave us an opportunity to see places of interest along the Grand Canal—the house where Byron died; the Rialto Bridge, made famous by Shakespeare; and the art galleries. A stop was made at the Church of Friars, where we saw a number of noted sculptures, woodcarvings, and paintings. Indeed, no amateur dares attempt to describe the precious works of famed artists, everywhere to be seen in Venice. Again, we stopped at a medieval palace, which needs a Sabatini to picture.

We saved the most important sights for the afternoon. We climbed the Campanile and viewed Venice, the wonderful, from the top of this age-old rebuilt tower; we visited Saint Mark's Cathedral, where we gazed upon priceless mosaics and paintings; and with considerable awe we stood before a great, unexploded bomb that was dropped by an enemy aeroplane during the World War but failed to go off—a miracle, we were told by a devout attendant.

Our next logical stop was at the Doge's Palace, where our eyes grew confused by the profusion of beauty, with the myriad paintings that decorated the walls, with the shining armor and gleaming swords. Of course, we paused to feed and watch the pigeons

Around the World at Seventeen

in the Saint Mark's Square; and gaze up at the Tower Clock, where a mechanical iron man wielding a sledge-hammer, struck the hour on the great gong.

I have omitted a multitude of details; after all, why undertake to describe the indescribable! The day was a full one, and we went aboard the *Ryndam*, tired but content, to sail for Trieste.

CHAPTER TWENTY-FIVE

Before leaving Venice the ship's officials, with an eye on the weather, foresaw an encounter with a stiff winter wind at Trieste. This wind is the dreaded Bora. Stories of its force are not exaggerated. During one of its fits of fury a train was blown off the track, not a rare occurrence in the lower Rhone Valley. When it is at its height it is not unusual to stretch ropes along the streets in Trieste, by means of which the pedestrian maintains his equilibrium. Apparently, the Bora is an inevitable evil. A large land area, very cold in winter, lies to the north; nearer lie high, snow-capped mountains. Eastward across this land blows the dense, dry, cold air; from the Adriatic Sea to the south the air is moist and warm. When these two opposing elements meet, a cyclonic condition results.

Hence, when the *Ryndam* attempted to dock at Trieste, the wind was blowing a forceful, bitter cold blast. The ship quivered from stem to stern; still, the power of its engines prevailed—but for a moment only; when the gangway was lowered and workmen started to board the vessel, a mighty blast sent it reeling, the gangplank slipped its housing, and but for the workmen's agility, they would have plunged into

Around the World at Seventeen

the icy water. For two hours the ship battled a wind and finally succeeded in lashing itself to the dock with half a dozen rope hawsers.

Once we were made fast to the dock, Walter H. Sholes, American Consul at Trieste, came aboard with Professor Giulio Morpurgo, rector of the Royal University at Trieste. After being introduced by the former, Professor Morpurgo gave an address of welcome in Italian, on the promenade deck. Translated, in substance he said:

"At the moment of your entering our city, I am pleased to offer you, in the name of the Royal University of Trieste, a hearty welcome; happy to be able to salute in you the brothers of those valorous Americans who fought side by side with the heroic Italian army which for ever liberated this region from the foreign yolk.

"All honor to the American nation which, in order to create the executive brains that will one day be called upon to govern the destinies of your great country, with a broadminded outlook, sends you to visit the various countries of the world with the object of obtaining an intimate knowledge of their habits and customs and conducting and deducting therefrom such benefits as may one day prove advantageous to your country.

"Greetings to you representatives of the rising generation who have traveled far to clasp the hand of

Around the World at Seventeen

peoples on distant shores, thereby laying the foundation of a friendship which may one day result in the unifying of the interests of the civilized world and thus make for the consolidation of universal peace. Welcome to the City of Trieste!"

I am calling attention to this address as it comes near striking the keynote of the cruise. We saw little of Trieste as we walked through ice-bound streets for a mile to the railroad station, to board the train for Postumia. Here we were to visit the famous Grottos.

The journey was uneventful, the train passing through a country of snow and ice, very much like Vermont in winter. Another two mile walk took us to the Grottos. Here we waited at the entrance for two hours and a half before the attendants arrived and opened the padlocked gates. Any one who has visited Mammoth Cave or the more recently discovered ones at Carlsbad has an idea of what the Grottos look like. The only thing of interest to me was the street car line which carried the sightseer to the famous underground chambers, operated much as ore cars in a mine.

We were ravenously hungry after our six mile hike through the snow and succeeded in getting an order of scrambled eggs at a little restaurant near the railroad station. After this treat, we went aboard the *Ryndam* and sailed for Malta.

After three days at sea the *Ryndam* dropped an-

Around the World at Seventeen

chor in the bay at Valetta and we went ashore in tenders. Once again, we were back in the Orient, with its heat; and I can vouch that Valetta is the dustiest city on the earth. Yet, it has the charm of a romantic past.

Tradition says the Apostle Paul stayed there long enough to convert the islanders to Christianity. Malta, with the Island of Gozo and Comino, lies 55 miles from Sicily and 185 miles from Africa. They evidently formed part of the last bridge that connected Africa and Europe, and sometime during the pluvial periods of the Ice Age, were flooded out by the extension of the Mediterranean Sea. Archeologically these islands are of great importance. Remains of megalithic temples, built by men of the New Stone Age, 30,000 years ago are numerous. The remains of hippopotami and elephants suggest, according to Dean Lough, that the advancing ice in northern Europe drove these beasts south into Africa, where elephants lived in the Atlas regions during Roman times. The islands were colonized about 150 B. C. by the Phœnicians; occupied by the Greeks in 750 B. C., and later by the Carthaginians. It was on the north coast of the Isle of Malta, in 62 A. D., that Saint Paul was shipwrecked.

But the most brilliant pages of the Island's history deal with the Order of the Knights of Malta. The order was founded at Jerusalem during the First Cru-

Around the World at Seventeen

sade; was expelled from the Holy Land by the Turks, after the fall of the Latin Kingdom in 1291. It was established in Rhodes and flourished there for 200 years. Thence its activities shifted to Malta, and gallant Hospitalers defended the Island with great valor against the last attacks of the Turks. Finally, after an unceasing warfare against the infidel, the Turks, and the Corsairs from the Barbary coast, the crisis came when Sultan Suliman, the Magnificent, laid siege to the Island fortifications in 1565. The siege lasted four and a half months, and when the Turks withdrew the Knights were left with not more than six hundred men capable of bearing arms. A new city replaced the old and was named after the gallant leader, Valette.

The Knights remained masters of the Islands until 1798, at which time Napoleon, wishing to use Malta as his naval base in the Egyptian campaign, dispersed them and took possession. Three years later the English Navy occupied it, and has never relinquished possession, using it as the Mediterranean naval base.

Getting back to my personal activities, the group I was with drove to the Aula Magna of the University of Malta, where the Rector of the University, Doctor Thomas Agius, made a formal speech of welcome. Then we broke up into small groups, each one with a native student guide at its head, and visited the high spots in and around Valette. There was St. John's

Around the World at Seventeen

Cathedral with its high arched ceiling and decorated side chapels; next we visited the museum, with its great store of Stone and Middle Age relics; we viewed briefly the huge domed Musta Church, built by volunteer labor, where I climbed to the top for a comprehensive view of the downtown section of Valette; then came a fifteen minute ride to the Hypogeum of Hal-Saflieni, where we went back 4,000 years in the history of Man, for the Hypogeum is a temple of the Stone Age, thirty feet underground. Near by stands the ruins of Tarien Temple belonging to the same age. The perfect day was capped with a tea dance at the Casino Maltese, after which we sailed for Naples.

Captain Lieuwen steered the boat ten miles off its course to give us a closer view of the snow-clad Mt. Etna and Stromboli, and as we steamed through the Straits of Messina we had a good view of lower Italy and Sicily.

When the boat docked at Naples Robinson was waiting to meet us. The traditionally sunny city of Naples greeted us with dripping skies and streets sticky with yellow mud. Slickers were in demand and we hastened to the waiting cars for the conventional drive about the city. It is the largest city in Italy, and with its murky shops and cobblestone streets, reminded me of Constantinople. Despite the rain, bedraggled children peered at us from doorways, the fishmongers displayed their wares on damp boards, while the fruit stands with their bright yellow oranges and dull yellow bananas made the only break in the drab color scheme.

We lunched at Cambrinus, a justly famous restaurant, crescent shaped and fronting three streets. Brown bread only, the finest I ever tasted, was served, Mussolini having placed a ban on white bread.

We resumed our drive in the afternoon but the rain discouraged us from getting out at the various points of interest. Even the Monastery of St. Martino held no attraction when viewed through a curtain of gray moisture, and the famous Gastel dell 'Ovo was drab and forbidding.

After the drive, Patterson and I wandered through the shopping district, and came upon the famous Arcade. This structure houses scores of shops. It consists of four wings centering under a great glass dome, with four corridors as wide as ordinary streets. The shops here were truly wonderful, the displays excelling anything I saw in Paris. Naples is famed for the manufacture of Borsolino hats, quite as well known as the Stetson in our country, and if anything finer.

Leaving the shopping center we wandered through devious streets to the cliff, at which point we viewed the city and bay, and the base of Vesuvius, the summit being obscured in the rain clouds.

Having seen Naples from this point, one is sup-

Around the World at Seventeen

posed to be ready to die, but the murky, dripping *vista* strengthened my desire to live on until I could once more find a sunny land.

The next day we boarded the dinky train for Pompeii. My failure to wax eloquent over the famous ruined city is due perhaps to the unfavorable weather conditions. So much has been written about Pompeii and its former grandeur, its distinctive architecture, and its art, that a mere enumeration of the various excavated edifices is all that is left one. In Malta, we saw ruins so much older and more significant in the relation they bore to the early history of Man that I viewed Pompeii with curiosity rather than respect. Guides conducted us through the ruins, interpreting the signs and symbols where the story of the spirit of the once buried city was not clear to the casual eye. I noted the brilliant red color in many of the houses which one always associated with Pompeii, as brilliant, no doubt, to-day, as when it was painted into the plaster. Seeing Pompeii from under an umbrella, in a drizzle of rain, dampens the enthusiasm of all but the most ardent archeologist.

We approached Rome under the most unpropitious conditions. The *Ryndam* dropped anchor in the harbor of Civitavecchia, the seaport of the Eternal City. The boat rode in a choppy sea, with a fierce wind blowing. At eight a.m., the entire cruise lined up to embark in the tenders. The process was not

Around the World at Seventeen

without its danger. As the tender drew alongside the ladderway, rolling heavily from side to side, two sailors stood ready to grab the passenger the moment the signal was given for him to jump. In this wise, with the wind freezing cold, the cruise managed finally to reach the dock about ten o'clock. There followed an uncomfortable walk of a mile to the station. So disagreeable was the weather that no one was abroad in the streets of Civitavecchia. We were obliged to wait five hours at the station before we boarded the train for Rome, fifty miles distant, and so slow was our progress that we did not arrive until nine p.m. I put up at the Romana hotel, and shortly after, Mrs. Robinson, Paul's mother, took Patterson, Killick, Paul, and myself to dinner—real home cooking. The head waiter was a beaming negro from Oklahoma, who received us with open arms. During the dinner, he entertained us by dancing the Charleston and otherwise showing his joy at beholding folk from home.

The next day the cruise was supplied with automobiles, my group of four drawing a new Fiat sedan. We first drove to the Vatican Museum which is filled with gifts to the Pope from the nations, as well as individuals, of the world—agate pedestals, finely carved tables, mosaics, and tapestries. The ceiling and walls are covered with fine paintings. In the Sistine Chapel

Around the World at Seventeen

we saw the Creation of the World and the Last Judgment by Michelangelo.

St. Peter's Cathedral, the largest in the world with its dome one hundred feet in diameter, was next visited. Some of the most interesting objects were the gold and bronze canopies, the colossal figures of the Fathers of the Church supporting the chair of St. Peter, and the statue of St. Peter, with the toe worn smooth from being kissed by worshipers. In a little marble niche, drawings were made to show the relative size of St. Peter's with the Cathedral of Milan, the one at Colon, and Santa Sophia.

We then went to the Pantheon, which puts one in mind of the sub-treasury in Wall Street; the Colosseum, similar to the Roman Theater we saw in Athens. There was once a shortage of iron in Rome and people chiseled great hunks of the metal from the girders that supported the ancient structure. Later we visited the Protestant Cemetery, where stand the tombs of Shelley and Keats.

Modern buildings were everywhere, the people well dressed and full of energy. A rather amusing thing occurred after we finished the automobile drive and continued our sightseeing on foot. At every corner a policeman whistled me down. I thought it was a warning to step lively. Finally it dawned on me that every one else was walking in an opposite direction;

Around the World at Seventeen

even the sidewalks were under one-way traffic law.

The outstanding event of our four days' stay at Rome was the audience granted the cruise by Premier Mussolini. At the entrance to the Chigi Palace stood huge Fascist guards, who eyed each entrant closely. These fellows are the most faithful of body guards. I am sure that if any one harbored a thought harmful to Benito Mussolini, he would be cut down on the spot. Before entering the palace we were again subjected to a close scrutiny by the guards. Then we ascended a carpeted spiral stairway, in groups of ten, confronted at every turn by more watchful guards, finally to enter the presence of Il Duce. Several persons not of the cruise endeavored to pass Dean Heckel and Dean Howes, but were detected and forced to turn back.

Premier Mussolini stood in the fourth room through which our line passed. Ex-governor Allen, standing beside him, introduced us to him. Il Duce is a short man, rather sturdily built, with a countenance inexorably stern. Mr. Fletcher, our ambassador, was also present. No sooner did Mussolini shake my hand with a low murmured word and the flash of a smile, than he turned to the next in line. Yet, in this fleeting glance I sensed the personality of the man. Whatever others may think of him, he thinks of himself as a man of destiny. I quote two of his utterances: "Italy is in our hands and we swear to

RECEPTION BY MUSSOLINI AT CHIGI PALACE

Around the World at Seventeen

lead her back into the ways of her ancient greatness." And again: "A man may move from a hut to a palace provided he can as easily move from the palace to a hut."

On our last day in Rome we drove to the top of the Seven Hills where we viewed the ancient Roman Forum with its ruins in a better state of preservation than those we found in Greece.

Instead of returning to Civitavecchia to embark on the *Ryndam*, we took the train for Naples, where the boat, due to rough weather, had sailed to meet us. After an all-night ride we arrived at Naples at seven a.m., boarded the boat, breakfasted and went to bed, to rest up for the trip to the Riviera.

CHAPTER TWENTY-SIX

The French Riviera! Always I had heard of the famous Continental playground without quite knowing what the term embraced. We had our first view when the *Ryndam* nosed into the Harbor of Villefranche; a panorama of French villages along a cliff-lined shore as far as the eye could see—villages of white, villas of white, cream and pink, bathing beaches lapped by white, foam-crested waves, parks set edgewise on greening hillslopes, winding drives, the whole picture framed in the blue of the sky and the blue of the Mediterranean.

The Riviera extends in this land of white and green and blue from Menton to Cannes, and nearly to Toulon, including Nice, Villefranche, and numerous less well known villages. Monaco is a tiny principality in which the profits of the Casino obviate the need of taxes.

Before going to Monte Carlo, Patterson, Killick, Robinson and I drove over the Petite Corniche, the famous mountain thoroughfare rebuilt by Napoleon I, in 1806, along the old Roman Road. It winds in and out, up and down, along the crags and cliffs of the Cote d'Azur. Clouds dipped down to encompass us; the ocean breeze fanned our faces with a chill

Around the World at Seventeen

breath, the world lay at our feet. Castles above us, villas below us, and further below, we beheld the tile roofs of the villages, in vivid colors, with tiny gardens everywhere.

Summed up, the Riviera is no place for the tourist. I got the impression that prices are exorbitant, and if one exclaims at the robber's rates, he is curtly asked why he is there if he has not plenty of money. The entire Riviera seems an endless procession of expensive cars, well-dressed men and women, fashionable villas, bathing beaches; and an outstanding expression of luxury and wealth is found in Monte Carlo. Although, I am told, you can live as moderately on the Riviera as anywhere.

Monte Carlo is distinctive in itself, a combination of beauty and vice, luxury and pitiful poverty. The poverty is that of character, men and women who have drained the Cup of Life until only the dregs remain, and in brilliant surroundings, to the click of the roulette ball and the monotonous drone of the croupier's voice, strive to win from Life one more thrill. That is the story one sees written on the pasty countenances of the habitués. Of course, there, too, is the sightseer who stakes a few francs, merely for the fun of the thing.

The present Casino of Monte Carlo was founded in 1853, by Francois Blanc, after a ban was placed on roulette gambling in Germany. It is a costly and

Around the World at Seventeen

ornate edifice, surrounded by perfectly kept grounds. It was built in 1878, from the plans of Charles Garnier, the constructor of the Grand Opera House in Paris. The various gambling rooms have luxurious appointments. The extensive terraces, the upper one with a charming music pavilion, afford superb views of Monaco, the harbor, and a panorama embracing nearly the whole coast of Monaco, Menton, and the Italian Riviera, as far as Cape Ampegio. There is also a theater connected with the Casino where good concerts and passable operas are given.

Patterson, being of age, anticipated no trouble in gaining admittance to the Casino; furthermore, he had his passports with him. The law is very strict about permitting minors to enter, and Robinson, Killick, and I listened in silence to Patterson's prophecy that we would be thrown out bodily. But we decided we would "crash the gate" regardless of consequences. One did not come to Monte Carlo to study architecture or to pluck posies in the gardens. It was decreed that I should be the leader; if I got past the silk-hatted doorkeepers, the others stood a chance to do likewise. In I marched with the bored air of an habitué. "One moment, Monsieur, where is your passport?" I look blankly at my questioner. Passport? I fumble through my pockets; my face lights up and I smile engagingly. "Why, in changing clothes, I must have left my passport in the discarded

Around the World at Seventeen

suit." "Are you twenty-one, Monsieur?" I am offended and frown. "Do I look like a schoolboy?" To be sure not, but—I stalk majestically past, turn, and in my most dignified manner, inform the doorkeeper that I vouch also for my two friends. Presto! We had successfully "crashed the gate."

The scenes we saw in the gambling parlors have been described too often for me to take the time to enumerate here—poor and rich gathered about the tables, watching the drop of the ball that would indicate a loss or a winning; pasty-faced old ladies, seated with their notebooks and pencils, playing a system; blasé millionaires with stacks of thousand franc notes before them; women dressed in the height of fashion, wooing the fickle goddess; and travelers from all over the world having their fling. But all the while one is impressed by the boredom and greed.

We returned to the boat to dress for dinner at La Perroquet, a famous night club in Nice. While we dined we watched the *giggilos,* the paid dancing men, who are hired by old ladies as escorts.

The next day, Sunday, saw the beginning of the Mardi Gras. The sun was shining, people filled the benches that lined the avenues; every one was bubbling over with the play spirit. To ward against the hard putty confetti which reminds one of the wedding rice, we donned wire masks. The revelers in the parade swarmed around the hideous King Carnival

Around the World at Seventeen

who sat enthroned with his jester at his side. The bands played "Coo-coo." Nice would go wild celebrating the two remaining weeks before Lent. After three hours of the carnival, during which time we were literally plastered with confetti, we returned to the *Ryndam* to sail for Algiers.

Booth Tarkington's *The Plutocrat*, characterizes Algiers as being the place where resides "the king of smells." We no sooner had landed at the pontoon dock than we realized the aptitude of the phrase. Typical French cars were on hand to drive us to the native quarters. Here we got out for a walk through dirty streets that swarmed with filthy beggars—streets as narrow and crooked as those we found in Jerusalem. Shopkeepers, resembling black-hooded monks, crouched beside their doors. The streets were cobblestone, with an occasional kerosene lamp to guide the pedestrian through the dark alleyways at night.

As in all ports, we had both pleasant and unpleasant adventures—at least the novelty one encounters in these out-of-the-way places raises them to the dignity of adventures. We decided to taxi to the St. George hotel, with the prospect of an excellent dinner. We entered a taxi, typically French, and drove through narrow streets, past sullen Arabs, seated cross-legged in their stalls, their wares spread before them; past half naked artisans, crouching around fires hammer-

Around the World at Seventeen

ing copper into household articles; past crows of child beggars, who shrilled oaths at us when we passed them up with a wave of the hand. For three hours we continued in this roundabout way until finally we arrived at the St. George, high up on a hill, with sloping lawns and a view of the bay with the *Ryndam* riding at anchor. Robinson was the first to get out and as he opened the door, door and door frame went with him. The driver had played a trick on us. Probably some time before he had had an accident and he meant to make us pay for it. There in front of the hotel entrance, with dozens of people looking on, we argued over the price with the driver. When the rascal set up a cry for the *gens d'armes* we saw it was high time to effect a settlement and paid him ten dollars for his precious door. From the standpoint of price, the hotel was equally bad. After an hour's rest, we had tiffin, and another ten dollars was gone.

In order to recoup our losses, we decided to return to town on the street car. The distance you ride on these cars is determined by the color of the ticket you buy. As we had no way of knowing what station to name as our destination, we put our faith in yellow tickets. Barely were we seated when the car stopped and the motorman clanged his bell. He was barefooted and grouchy. The other passengers looked at us impatiently. We could see nothing wrong with our behavior or appearance, therefore we sat still.

Around the World at Seventeen

Finally the motorman came back to us and ordered us off; our yellow tickets had played us false. Thoroughly disgusted we decided to walk the remaining distance to town.

But a pleasant experience followed. At the Cunard Line office we obtained passes to visit the *Mauretania*, which we first saw in the harbor as we sailed into port. The *Mauretania* was the first ocean liner I had ever been on; it was like a huge hotel, with its elevators, swimming pools, gaming courts, ball rooms, and every convenience to insure comfort and luxury to its passengers.

In Algiers, too, we found the Mardi Gras in full swing, the streets alive with people, pickpockets doing a thriving business, and the whole town pleasure mad. While we wended our way through the crowds, watching the parade of grotesque figures and dodging the inevitable confetti, a huge Arab charged down upon us. Not being inclined to step aside, I gave him a stiff elbow, he recoiled with a fierce oath, flashed his sword and made at me again. The encounter began to look serious, and while I nimbly side-stepped the thrusts and passes of the irate Arab, I cast about for a means of escape. Just then the Arab laughed—a perfectly good English laugh—and slipped off his headpiece disclosing Dick Black, one of the cruise members.

Apropos of pickpockets, I had an experience with

Around the World at Seventeen

a dirty street urchin that makes me want to disinfect myself every time I think about it. I was ascending a narrow passageway when a shrill voice greeted me from above. I looked up at the young beggar and waved him aside. He shrilled an oath and launched himself full upon my back, his legs pinning my arms while with his free hands he began an energetic search of my pockets for money. Before he could find my billfold, however, I managed to free myself and flung him, shrieking and swearing, down the steps.

To say the least, Algiers is a colorful port. It was the center of the slave trade in the Mediterranean until the French captured it in 1830. The French accession of the province came about in a peculiar manner. During the days of Algerian independence, there were many outrages against the Christians. The French consul, protesting against a particularly atrocious manifestation of Moslem enthusiasm, so enraged the ruler that the latter struck the consul on the cheek with his hand. At this insult to French dignity, an invasion was ordered, resulting in Algeria becoming French territory.

I felt very much at home when we sailed into Malaga, for the Spanish town looked much like a diminutive Mexico City, except the Prado, which looks like Havana's, where the women walk in one direction and the men in the opposite. Here, too, I would be given another opportunity to try out my

Around the World at Seventeen

Spanish. There was a tacit understanding in my group that Robinson was our spokesman in French, Killick in Italian, while I made known our needs in Spanish. Our sightseeing in Malaga was done on foot. On our way we visited the Cathedral of Malaga, with its old choir stalls of elaborately carved wood, on the wall of every stall the figure of a saint. Further on we came to the bull ring, where the Spaniards foregather to enjoy the national sport. Finally we came upon the hillside behind the town, on the slope of which Gibralfaro Castle stands, a great rambling fortress, snow white against the blue of the sky. The others were in favor of going on to the top, but I decided the view from where I stood was pleasing enough. Left alone, I observed the most truly native scene of the cruise. Just below me was a typical Spanish peasant home with the housewife singing at her work. A youthful goatherd sauntered past me with his grazing charges. A conversation ensued, and the boy and I got on such familiar terms that he bummed me for a cigarette.

When my party returned to town, we adjourned to a little restaurant, where it so happened all the guests were Americans, mostly sailors from the boats in port, and a few cruise members. Apparently I was the only one present who spoke Spanish and I got quite a "kick" out of ordering the meals for all the guests, including my own party.

Around the World at Seventeen

In the afternoon Robinson and I hired a rickety carry-all and drove out along the bathing beach, now unfrequented because of the cold weather. The beach had stone walks extending far out into the breakers. We amused ourselves by following the receding breakers to the end of the walk and being chased back again by the succeeding one.

The Queen of Spain was a guest at the Hotel Principe de Asturias. At night she gave the cruise a reception and had the Globe Trotters, the student orchestra, play lively jazz music while Kelly Eikel and Jack Aiken danced the Charleston. So well did she like the dance that she commanded the Globe Trotters and Miss Eikel and Jack Aiken to be her personal guests for a week, during which time they gave exhibitions of the Charleston in all the important cities in Spain.

On the morning of Saturday, March 5, the 169th day of the cruise, we arose at four o'clock to board the train of baggage cars for the six hour ride to Granada, our destination being the most famous palace in the world, the Alhambra. The wind was biting cold, and the wooden benches hard, but we carried blankets, which we wrapped about us, and succeeded in being fairly comfortable. The route to Granada borders the Sierra Nevada Mountains and climbs steadily upward from the seashore. Past the fertile valley of Vega de Malaga, the scenery is wild and reminiscent of the holds of robbers. A sheer face of precipitous rock, with a rushing torrent at its base, is cleft as though by the stroke of a giant's knife. One tunnel follows another in rapid succession until finally the road emerges on a level, and Granada is reached.

All along in every available valley Spanish *haciendas* stand out snowy white against the drab Sierras. Innumerable farms, well kept and prosperous looking, cover the alluvial valleys. Despite the popular conception of the Spaniards' easy going habits, the natives, wherever we encountered them, were in a rush and bustle.

Paradoxically, we saw little of Granada until we got a general view of it from the summit of the hill upon which stands the Alhambra. Then Granada spread before us, a city of white, with vari-colored tile roofs. The road leading to the Alhambra passes through the Gate of the Pomegranates, mounts and winds through a thick wood to the ancient Gate of Justice, and finally brings the visitor to that gaunt reminder of the futility of Man's ambition, the gaping, never finished palace of Charles V. Beside it rises that miracle, the Alhambra. Mohammed I laid the foundation in 1250; but it was not finished until a century later by Mohammed V. It has been restored with the most painstaking care and a distinct idea of its original grandeur can be gained. It is ornate, in-

Around the World at Seventeen

credibly elaborate, but exquisitely delicate for all that.

A slow drizzle of rain drenched us and shivering with cold we wandered through its halls and courts. Just outside the door and in keeping with the depressing weather, an old blind beggar mournfully sang his lay. The sunny Spain of Washington Irving was lacking, although, despite the atmospheric conditions, the brilliant colored tiles in some of the rooms inspired one with their beauty.

We left the Alhambra to follow the road up the hill to the pleasure house of the former kings, the Generalife. Gardens with flowing fountains, terraced grounds, and stately cypress trees welcomed us despite the foggy drizzle of rain. From the windows of the Generalife, the River Darro was seen, winding its way through the countryside.

We adjourned to the Washington Irving Hotel, situated below the Alhambra, and there we were revived with good hot coffee, which fortified us for the five hour train ride back to Malaga and the *Ryndam*.

CHAPTER TWENTY-SEVEN

Our next port of call was Gibraltar. I had always associated the great rock with the Prudential Life Insurance Company. Strategically, it is perhaps the most strongly situated fortress in the world, but it stands out less conspicuously than the Diamond Head near Honolulu. We docked and went ashore for a brief walk through the town, but got no closer view of the honeycombed fortification, due to the strict regulations governing admission to the fortress. The city itself is nondescript, with a total population, including the military, of about 20,000. British currency is legal, but Spanish coins are accepted. On the Spanish shore opposite is Algeciras, and the point on the African coast where now stands the Spanish town of Ceuta formed, with Gibraltar, what the ancients knew as the "Pillars of Hercules." We reached Gibraltar on Sunday and all the stores were ostensibly closed, but Bill Worthington and I managed to inveigle a merchant into selling us a few necessary things to carry on shipboard.

The next day we passed the point of St. Vincente and once again were in Atlantic waters. We passed up Cadiz, the most beautiful of the Spanish seaports, due to a change in the cruise itinerary, and continued

Around the World at Seventeen

on to Lisbon, the capital of Portugal. In these later days, one hears very little of this once great maritime country. Lisbon, with a population of approximately 800,000, stands on the northern bank of the Tagus river, about seven miles from its mouth, where it widens into a natural harbor. Legend attributes the founding of Lisbon to Ulysses, and as if following in his footsteps, the inhabitants of this little country have given the world many notable explorers, merchantmen, and not a few of the most notorious sea rovers.

When we landed, we saw evidence of a fitful revolution that had swept the town the week before. Many of the buildings were riddled from machine gun fire, houses with a dozen windows fronting the street had not a single window-pane intact, expensive plateglass in shop fronts was demolished, and belfries and cupolas that evidently screened sharp-shooters were completely shot away.

Lisbon lies out of the path of the tourist; prices are sky high, and there is no bid for this lucrative source of trade in the bustling commercial city. Yet, there are a number of things of interest in the capital. Due to its hilliness, elevators carry the pedestrian from one street level to another. It was the busiest port we had visited. Thousands of ships rode at anchor in the harbor and the dock front reminded me of North River, New York. The architecture of

Around the World at Seventeen

the public buildings and churches seems to be a conglomeration of the ideas infused by the various masters of this much conquered land, the Jeronumous Church being a splendid example of the heterogeneous mixture, with its twisted Byzantine columns reaching up into a Gothic arch. This church is built in the form of a Latin cross; in the chapel of one of the arms of the cross, there is the cross and the figure of the Savior, which formerly stood on the bank of the river in full sight of the departing navigators. The last act of every Portuguese sailor, before he nosed his boat around Calha Point and headed for the open sea, was to offer up a hastily whispered prayer to this Christ.

We spent the most of two days at Lisbon but I refrained from making purchases on account of the high prices. I did find a little Swiss restaurant, however, which I thoroughly enjoyed. When we steamed out of the Tagus, past Belem Castle, our thoughts turned to the forthcoming visit to the most talked of city in the world—Paris.

An imperceptible change had been taking place in the University Afloat since our arrival in Mediterranean waters. Due to so many of the students meeting relatives on the Riviera and in Paris and continuing on with them, class-room work was disorganized. On sailing from Lisbon there remained a total of twenty days at sea between us and New York; the

Around the World at Seventeen

remainder of the time, consisting of thirty-two days, was to be given over to visiting the dozen remaining ports and inland cities scheduled by the cruise management. Therefore, a few days more of class work and our exams would complete our year's college work.

Hitherto, I have endeavored to recount the events of the cruise in which I participated in chronological order. In the remaining thirty-two days ashore, our progress from place to place and from one point of interest to another was so rapid; our haste was so great and we were so eager to see everything, that my notes and log-book jottings became slightly scrambled. If the reader desires to try a difficult experience, let him hie himself to Paris, for instance, hit the pace day and night, and endeavor meanwhile to keep accurate notes on his itinerary. I am quite sure he will be fortunate if he remembers half the things he did.

After the four days at sea, and the forenoon of the fifth spent drifting in the English Channel; and after Captain Lieuwen received the fifth signal from passing ships asking if he were in distress, we cleared the quarantine and docked at Le Havre in the late afternoon, a day ahead of schedule.

Le Havre is the largest of the French ports in the English Channel, and is the only one capable of accommodating large trans-Atlantic steamers. During

Around the World at Seventeen

the World War, it was the main supply depot of the British armies in France.

A cold stiff March wind was blowing, but despite the raw weather there was a general rush for the trains to Paris. I kept to the boat, however, the first evening, spending the time packing for my five days' stay in Paris. The next morning Killick, Robinson and I boarded the seven o'clock train for the queen of cities. We all know people who say they do not like New York, or London, or Chicago; but if there breathes a human being who does not like Paris, he keeps it a dark secret. As we taxied along the boulevards to the hotel assigned us, I confess the distinctive Parisian atmosphere charmed me.

I know a chap who had a two hour stop over at the Pennsylvania Station, New York, before he proceeded on his journey. He has talked about New York ever since. My five days in Paris left me rather breathless and with little to say. Summed up, there is the Paris of the Louvre, and the Paris of the Montmarte. Almost every one takes a fling at both; I did.

After we were comfortably settled at a typical French hotel, we taxied downtown in search of food. A large electric sign indicated "Sam's Place." We went no further and were rewarded by a good American-cooked lunch. I suppose every American in Paris knows "Sam's Place"; no French is spoken and you can order anything from Post Toasties to *chile*

Around the World at Seventeen

and coffee with real cream. It was one of our favorite hangouts during our stay in Paris.

After being thoroughly satiated with the Orient, it was good to drop downstairs to Harry's New York Bar, with its real American atmosphere, eat real American food and listen to Bill Henly sing the latest song hits while Bud Shepherd played the piano.

Much like New York, Paris has its subway, and every car apparently is a taxi. If I wanted to get somewhere in a hurry, I took the former; if time hung heavily on my hands, I taxied through the boulevards, or the Boulevard de la Madeleine and the beautiful Champs Elysées; or through the Rue de la Paix, the most exclusive shopping street in the world, where one sees signs in English of well-known American and British firms; or to the Louvre, with its miles of galleries, and artists and students seated at easels copying from the old masters.

Another good way to pass the time, in the mornings between ten and noon, is to repair to the American Express Company's office, where every one goes —especially after a night spent in sightseeing and revelry—to refill their depleted purses. Watching the crowd there, one is almost sure to meet an acquaintance or a friend, who perhaps has been lost sight of temporarily.

Of course, there are the Avenue de l'Opera, the Place de l'Etoile, the Place de la Concorde, the Tuile-

Around the World at Seventeen

ries Gardens, Notre Dame, and the Eiffel Tower. I omit mention of scores of places just as interesting as these. The most restful scenes on the trip, I think, were witnessed as I lolled in a taxi driven slowly past the numerous open-air cafés, with me watching the old-timers chat and smoke over their coffee.

Thoughts of the World War, although ten years has passed, were ever in one's mind in Paris. All cruise members who were in Paris took the trip to the battlefields—Belleau Wood, the Marne and Château-Thierry. We motored along well-paved, tree-lined highways for some distance. The countryside grew harsher in appearance as we approached the battlefields, where the erosion from deforestation was heavy; the old forests, now replaced by groves of young trees, had been literally wiped out by gunpowder. Everywhere reclamation was going on rapidly. We stopped at villages where scarcely a house had a wall intact; churches with their roofs and belfries shot away—these signs of war's devastation stood grim reminders of the great calamity in well kept, greening fields. At Oise-Aisne we visited the thousands of graves that marked the last resting place of our boys who fell in the world struggle. Many of the graves were nameless. In the French cemetery we saw the plain white crosses over the Frenchmen's graves; and slabs surmounted by white stars for the Algerian troops of the Mohammedan

Around the World at Seventeen

faith. We stood reverently, with bared heads, about the little fence that railed in the grave of Quentin Roosevelt. The slab has this simple inscription: "On this spot fell Quentin Roosevelt, son of ex-President Roosevelt, July 14, 1918. Erected as a memorial by the 302nd Engineers." The Germans buried him on the spot his plane had fallen, with full military honors.

The next day, the cruise assembled at the Arc de Triomphe, to place a wreath on the grave of the Unknown Soldier. There were speeches by several French generals and Ambassador Herrick, while Jim Price, President of the Student Council, spoke in behalf of the students.

I was much alone in Paris; the others were occupied with dinners, dancing and receptions tendered them by friends and relatives who were visiting or residing in the city. But I enjoyed every moment of my stay. As an onlooker I visited the more fashionable night clubs, cabarets, theaters, and revues. The Paris of the Bright Lights was created by and for the tourist, and no American, whether he is a steady business man or of sporting blood, misses this phase of life in the capital of capitals. On my farewell ride in the subway, for a last visit to the Place de l'Opera, before boarding the train for Brussels, I resolved I would again visit Paris for a longer stay.

CHAPTER TWENTY-EIGHT

To Americans, who are accustomed to traveling days in one direction on fast trains, without even approaching our borders, the smallness of the European countries is brought home forcibly. Our next forty-eight hours were spent in three different countries, leaving France, passing through Belgium, entering Holland. As all signs in Belgium are in French, my entrance to the little Kingdom was unheralded by any change, but I knew I was in Holland when the signs became Dutch.

To avoid confusion I will take up Belgium and Holland in proper order. We left Paris shortly after noon, passing through village after village, with intervals of countryside between, where the effects of the late war were still to be seen, especially in the St. Quentin sector. The town of St. Quentin was almost a ruin, with the chimneys shot away, walls of houses agape where shells struck, and shell holes everywhere. Still, there has been much rebuilding there.

We arrived in Brussels in time for a late dinner but were too tired to attempt seeing the city by night. The next morning early, however, we climbed aboard the "rubber-neck" busses for a visit to the battle mound at Waterloo. The outskirts of Brussels im-

Around the World at Seventeen

pressed me as being the most attractive place to live we had yet encountered on the cruise. The wide brick highway over which we drove was lined with beautiful homes; the air was cold and bracing and there was an orderliness about the estates and farms that appeals to any one with the least appreciation of the neat. The memorial at Waterloo is a pyramidal mound with a square monument rising from the apex surmounted by the figure of a lion. From this monument, one can see Brussels, eighteen kilometers away. At the base of the pyramid, in a miniature pantheon, is a panorama of the battle of Waterloo, done in *papier-mâche*.

Returning to Brussels, Bob Long and I decided we would fly to Rotterdam, but unfortunately it was Sunday and we found the ticket offices closed. We whiled the time away driving about the city and boarded the train for Rotterdam in the afternoon.

The *Ryndam* had preceded us to Rotterdam, the home port of the Holland America Line, where it would undergo repairs before continuing the voyage that would end in New York. After six months aboard the Dutch ship we were well acquainted with the Dutch crew, their traditions, dispositions, and way of doing things. So that now we approached Holland not entirely as strangers, but as friends paying a visit to a friendly country. We had heard the crew talk a great deal about their home country and we looked forward eagerly to seeing what it was like. If I fail to convince the reader that our anticipation was met with one hundred per cent fulfillment then I am to blame, not the Dutch.

Signs written in Dutch informed us that we had entered Holland. On all sides were greening fields, silver canals, a country so level that one gets the impression it was planed and shaved. As night drew on, the distinctive tower windmills of Holland sent out welcoming twinkles of light from their windows, suggesting the family within at the evening meal, while the arms of the mills turned slowly on. These windmills are both artistic and utilitarian; they are the homes of the farmer families; they pump the water from the rivers to the canals or reclaim the low lands by giving the water back to the sea, they grind the farmer's flour and are the power plant to numerous small industries. There were no two of them alike, and they were scattered along the countryside or in the squares of the villages through which our speeding train passed.

We arrived at the station in Rotterdam and went immediately to the ship for dinner and to freshen up. In the United States, every home, no matter how humble, has its bathroom, and bathing is an everyday occurrence. With Europeans it is almost a ritual. To take a bath in a European hotel involves as much red tape and effort as one undergoes to get a railroad

Around the World at Seventeen

pass or a free ticket to a ball game in our country. As a special enticement to prospective patrons, a European hotel will advertise that it has a bathroom. This may not be true of the Ritz and other palatial hostelries, but it holds good with the smaller hotels of Europe. Once one has gone through the formalities of ordering his bath, however, he finds it of the best. He is furnished with a slip-on bath-robe in which he is led to the bathroom. You leave all your clothes behind; but do not forget your pocketbook. You tip one person for turning the water into the tub; you pay another for bringing the soap; another for bringing the towels; and finally after you are safely back in your room, you tip the person who comes to inquire if everything was all right. Needless to say, I thoroughly enjoyed my tipless bath once I got aboard the *Ryndam*.

With Rotterdam as our operating center for the next four days, we managed to see a good deal of Holland, including the Hague and Delft. The cruise was tendered a number of formal receptions by the universities and various civic bodies. Holland we found to be modern in every particular. In Rotterdam many of the street railways were elevated and everybody spoke English. Window decorations in the downtown shops were futuristic in effect, the displays luring the onlooker from behind thick plate-glass. Everywhere one went he was seated on strangely

Around the World at Seventeen

carved chairs, sometimes representing the back of a stork with the head thrust to one side, or a chicken, or some sort of animal. We were in the homeland of the stork, but the lanky, long-necked bird seemed not to possess the symbolism that we in the United States give it.

Rotterdam lies on both banks of the Nieuwe Maas, eighteen miles from the sea. It is the first receiving port for the products of the Dutch East Indies, also for the industries and coal mines of Western Germany. It is intersected by numerous canals which serve to connect the port with Germany, Belgium, and the interior of Holland. Our second days stay was filled with group trips. Patterson and I went pretty much together. In the morning, we boarded a tender for a trip up the Nieuwe Maas, to the center of the oleomargerine industry. These factories furnish London, among other great cities, with oleo and butter. Here, likewise, we found large coffee and tobacco manufactures, and we returned to Rotterdam very much impressed with the commercial activities of the Dutch.

Delft, famous the world over for the Delftware tile, and tableware, was visited. The city is just like the name sounds, clean, wholesome smelling, with concrete pavements and the water of the canals gleaming green and clear, and barges pushed along with poles or drawn by well-fed horses along the

Around the World at Seventeen

bridlepaths traversing the length of the rock-rimmed banks. We visited a number of these tile factories and I regretted not being able to send a shipment home. Every one is familiar with Delft tableware and we saw some exquisite designs.

A visit to the Hague followed, the city made famous by the World Peace Conferences. The Hague has a population of eight hundred thousand people and four hundred thousand bicycles. Everybody rides bicycles; I was reminded of Japan. We visited the Peace Palace, a magnificent structure built in the style of the Dutch Renaissance. Here were displayed the gifts of all nations—Oriental tapestry and porcelains, and many European art treasures. The work of the Flemish masters covered the walls of the throne room with their voluptuous beauty, and the tapestries were made of real bird feathers and animal skins, strikingly unusual.

On the morning of the third day, a special train took us to Amsterdam, called by many, "The Venice of the North," because of its network of canals. Amsterdam is just as modern as the other Dutch cities we had visited, and there was disappointment expressed by the cruise members that we had not seen the quaint Dutch costumes, the wooden shoes, and the starched caps, which we in America so closely associate with the Dutch. But we were in for a pleasant surprise, when we visited the Isle of Marken and

Around the World at Seventeen

Vollendam. Here, we found all the customs and quaintness of Holland, here the picturesque caps, wooden shoes, wide skirts, and baggy pantaloons are worn by the inhabitants, under a decree of the Government. Furthermore, we found prices reasonable and we had a wonderful lunch at a little inn where the register disclosed the signatures of many kings, potentates and celebrities—Napoleon, Charlie Chaplin, and Jack Dempsey, for instance.

Before returning to Rotterdam, we took a ride through the streets of Amsterdam, visited the sea wall and the amusement pier and the paved promenade lined with fashionable hotels, reminding me very much of Atlantic City.

While in Amsterdam, I had the satisfaction of completing arrangements with the American Express Company, whereby Dick Kerckhoff and I mapped out an aeroplane tour of Germany, via Cologne. We were fortunate in that Kerckhoff spoke German fluently and we anticipated an interesting flight.

Our meandering back and forth between Rotterdam and Amsterdam may be confusing to the reader; suffice to say we returned a second time to Amsterdam to begin our flight over Germany. Familiar as I was with the numerous large military and flying fields at San Antonio, I was dumbfounded at my first view of the huge airport to which the Royal Dutch Air Line bus conveyed us after picking us up at our hotel.

Around the World at Seventeen

While we were yet four miles away, the hum of motors filled our ears. When we arrived at the flying field we saw scores of concrete hangars and the field itself was literally alive with planes, the largest and most luxurious I had ever seen. The Royal Dutch Air Line radiates to every important city in Europe; both monoplane and biplane types are used and carry ten, fifteen and more passengers each.

The bus drew up at the passenger station, where we bought our tickets and repaired to the waiting room. All the airport equipment is complete and represents the last word in comfort. Presently, a "red cap" escorted us to a huge glassed-in biplane, and we were soon comfortably seated in the passengers' salon. We were the only passengers. The plane was divided into three compartments—one for the two pilots, a larger one for the passengers, and a small wash room. The salon was equipped with electric fans, eight wicker stuffed chairs, and the interior woodwork was done in gray enamel. Although the weather was cold, an electric radiator kept us snug and warm. Our pilots next came aboard, saluted and took their places, shouted the German equivalent for, "Contact!" and we took off. Our take-off was devoid of bumps and the usual roar of the propeller; there was only a slight vibration and we quickly reached the altitude of a thousand feet, straightened out, and sped on our way.

Kerckhoff and I settled back comfortably to gaze

Around the World at Seventeen

down at the wonderful bird's-eye view that spread below us. Holland, from the air, appeared a network of canals. These canals cut the green landscape into parallelograms. As we mounted to a higher altitude the country looked like a big lake, so numerous were the canals. We flew over Rotterdam, Hague, and Delft, ever on the lookout for the Rhine, which would mark our entrance to Germany. Finally in the distance we saw the river, like a silver ribbon strung across the earth. The obliging pilot dipped the plane and for a distance flew along the Rhine's course. We hovered so low that we could distinguish the Germans sipping their beer on the numerous pleasure boats that plied the river. Then we mounted again, leaving the Rhine, and approached the Black Forest district. Here we flew over one town after another, and the country became hilly, rising to low mountain tops and falling into valleys. The pilot raised and dipped the plane, skimming like a bird. In the distance, we saw the smoke of an immense factory, the home of the Krupp industry, and soon we circled down to the fine stadium of the Luft Hansa Air Line, at Essen.

Here we drank a cup of coffee while our passports were examined and our luggage changed to a monoplane. This second ship was smaller, with one pilot, but just as luxurious as the first. At the cry of, "Contact!" in German, we took off with greater

Around the World at Seventeen

speed than the first time. Up, up, we mounted. We must have been flying two hundred miles an hour. The pilot, anticipating a storm, shot his plane up through the clouds, to gain altitude. It grew suddenly dark; a flash of lightning blinded our eyes, and a crash of thunder deafened our ears; then it began to rain, the torrent beating down on the wings sounding like the patter on a tin roof. The storm quickly passed—or rather we passed it—and the pilot directed the plane to a lower altitude. Here we flew low over green fields and valleys. At first I thought we were being forced down because of engine trouble; we began to circle and before I realized it we were landed at the stadium of another Luft Hansa airport, at Cologne.

CHAPTER TWENTY-NINE

WE stepped from the wing of our plane to the waiting bus and were driven to the railroad station, where we had a late lunch, discussing meanwhile the impressions of our recent flight. The whole trip including the bus service, our coffee, and a light lunch, with which we started from Amsterdam, cost us the reasonable sum of eight dollars each. But what surprised us most was the unconcern with which passengers board their planes, accidents apparently being unthought of, the as yet novel mode of travel being already accepted as an ordinary occurrence.

Cologne is known the world over for its perfume factories; also, it has the third largest cathedral in the world, a stately pile of Gothic architecture. The buildings of the town appeared old and grimy in the downpour of rain, and we tarried but a short while, anxious as we were to reach Heidelberg in time to gain a few hours' rest after our strenuous day.

Boarding the train for Frankfort, and after making three changes, we arrived at the famous German university city at two o'clock in the morning. There were many Heidelberg students on board the train who kept up a constant racket, reminding me of students at home returning from a football game.

Around the World at Seventeen

A hotel porter met the train and conducted us to the Heidelberg Hotel.

The next morning, after a late breakfast, we strolled through the streets. Heidelberg is a town of souvenirs, sausage factories, delicatessen shops, and rosy-cheeked people. But we saw no scarred-faced, dueling students, nor venerable college walls.

When finally we found the university, we failed to recognize it as such. It consisted of several old buildings, with half the window-panes broken out, at the corner of the two intersecting streets, with no sign of a campus. We encountered two boys, who spoke English and proved to be under-graduates. They kindly volunteered to escort us through the buildings. The lecture rooms were severe in appointments, the benches old and hard. We saw not a single modern touch, age apparently being the key-note upon which the university's fame rests. On the third floor of one of these gray buildings we were shown through the prison, where unruly students were once confined. It was a real dungeon keep; in a sense, an art gallery and library combined, for the student prisoners passed their time drawing cartoons and writing epigrams on the walls. There was a famous cartoon of Bismarck, pictures of the Kaiser, and more recent cartoons of Americans with donkey ears, results, I suspect, of the late World War.

While an anti-dueling law was passed several years

ago, only last year the university authorities began to enforce it. But we saw the court yards where the duels were fought. The man with the most scars was prominent in student and fraternity activities. In order to make their wounds gape, the student duelist rubbed salt in the slashes. A duelist's prominence was not due to his victories, but to the number of scars he bore.

On the whole we were not much impressed with the University of Heidelberg, outside of the "art collection," and we left the "campus" to climb a steep hill, where on the brow of a precipice, surrounded by a black forest, stood the ruins of Heidelberg Castle. We each paid an attendant one mark to show us through. In the wine cellar stood the largest wine barrel in the world, the top serving for a dance pavilion. The attendant told us it had been filled three times and pipes from the huge container ran to all the rooms, somewhat in the manner ice-water is conveyed through a modern building. We had a wonderful view of the Rhine River from the castle walls, and the grounds were beautiful and well kept. Before leaving the grounds we had a typical Dutch lunch at a little restaurant, for the sum of two marks. There we left our attendant and returned to the hotel for a brief rest before departing for Berlin.

When I arrived in Berlin I drove straight to the hotel on the Fredrickstrasse designated by the cruise

Around the World at Seventeen

management. The Ryndamers were to arrive at noon and I spent the time, meanwhile, strolling up and down the famous Unter den Linden, past the university with its famous library, the palace of former Kaiser Wilhelm II, the Kaiser galleries, the Academy of Art facing the Pariser Platz, and through the "Versailles of Berlin"—the Tiergarten. It was Sunday and the Germans were out full force on dress parade, each one trailing a dog muzzled and leashed.

At noon Robinson, Killick, and Patterson joined Kerckhoff and me, and we repaired to a projection room where we amused ourselves running off the motion pictures Robinson had taken at the various ports.

Despite previous impressions of Germany's poverty-striken condition, flaunted in our faces by newspapers these past several years, I found in Germany's capital city a general air of prosperity, of hustle and bustle, of progress, that astonished me greatly. I was impressed and moved by the friendliness of the people, who seemed to have forgotten that we Americans were erstwhile foes, and played an important part in their losing the struggle for world dominance. Berlin is too large to describe; there is a touch here of New York and Paris, with the natives taking both their pleasure and business rather seriously. One has the feeling that the German plays hard that he may

Around the World at Seventeen

be enabled to work harder—efficiency in all things being the key-note to the German character.

I was two days in Berlin, little time enough to see even the principal attractions of one of the largest cities in the world. I was told there is a more hopeful outlook for republican Germany than there ever was for imperial Germany, and yet, everywhere, ghosts of the old régime confront one and I could not help but observe the reverence in which these reminders of the imperialistic past were held by the people of the new republic.

One of my last acts was to go to the British Consulate and get a special visa of my passport so that I might later on go from Leith to London by train. Then I spent four tedious hours traveling from Berlin to Hamburg, which city I reached thoroughly fatigued, and went aboard the *Ryndam* for the night.

With over a million population, Hamburg is the largest shipping port on the continent, and due to a cholera epidemic in 1892, sanitary conditions were improved to such an extent that it is one of the healthiest cities in Europe. One peculiarity I noted in Hamburg was its subway system. Starting from the center of the business district, the subway describes an ever increasing circle, like a spiral, as it reaches the outer confines of the city. Hamburg is a free port and her quays extend for six miles along the bank of the Norder-Elbe and accommodate thou-

Around the World at Seventeen

sands of ships and river crafts. While it is a great commercial and shipping center, Hamburg has gained recognition in the Arts. The first German theater for opera was founded there in 1677; and during the last century many fine collections such as those at the Kunstalle and the Arts and Crafts Museum have added to the interest of the city.

We left Amsterdam to make the northernmost swing of the cruise, where we would visit the three important Scandinavian cities. The first of these, Copenhagen, Denmark, we reached at early morn, but the report of our momentary quarantine in Italy had preceded us, and we were not allowed to land until noon.

A most depressing land, Denmark! The old Danish tradition tells how the god Gefion carved Denmark out of the Scandinavian Peninsula with a huge plow. The plowshare toppled clods into the water some distance from the shore, and one of these clods became the Island of Seland in Cattegat Sound. Here the Danes founded a small fishing village in 1043, and later the humble huts of the fisher folk grew into the capital of Denmark, Copenhagen. No wonder the suicide rate is so high; nowhere else could Shakespeare have found a more fitting character and environment for his *Hamlet*.

During our two days' stay, we visited Elsinore, and the Kornenberg Castle, standing bleak and dreary

Around the World at Seventeen

and mysterious on top of the fortified mound northeast of town; we saw the reputed grave of Hamlet, and Ophelia's brook babbling on its way, much as in the times about which Shakespeare wrote his tragedy. In walking through the grounds of the King's palace, Kerckhoff and I saw their majesties, the King and Queen of Denmark, drive past, while we stood at attention—a posture assumed at the insistence of the numerous guards to their majesties.

Our downtown explorations included two fine museums, one of which contains the work of the great sculptor, Thorwaldsen; the other a great assortment of gifts from every country in the world. In the latter, too, were Danish relics of early days, hunting weapons, great steins, and drinking horns—such crude but sturdy implements as might have been used by a race of giants. In every sense the city is modern. We walked through the lobby of the Hotel D'Angleterre, where the women guests smoked black cheroots with the same gusto, if with less dignity, than the French women their gold-tipped cigarettes. This, too, was a city of bicycles. Last and most impressive of all, was the huge crowd, probably ten thousand people, that followed the ship the length of the long mole, waving good-by, as the *Ryndam* pulled out to sea for the day's journey to Göteborg.

The ship was greeted at Göteborg by a downpour of rain, despite which the Ryndamers made the trip

Around the World at Seventeen

to Trollhatten. The way lay through mountains covered with spruce trees, many of which eventually find their way to the United States in the form of matches. We swept through cultivated valleys, along picturesque gorges, and tarried for a brief inspection of the large hydro-electric plant on the river Trollhatten. This huge generating plant supplies most of Sweden with light and power. We viewed Trollhatten Falls, where the river takes a great plunge. Here we again encountered the canals which were so numerous in these northern European countries. In the afternoon, a golden sun emerged from the clouds and put us all in better spirits. The weather was crisp and the scenery wherever we went was the sort one finds in Minnesota or Wisconsin. The Swedes are an energetic race; the farmhouses are substantial and the fields well tilled. The city of Göteborg, with its population of a quarter of a million, is the commercial, educational, and ship-building center of Sweden. It is a town of brick homes and wide streets, standing on both banks of the river Gotha, three miles from its mouth. Once back in the city, we were given a reception in the University of Göteborg and we sailed away, as we came, in a downpour of rain.

Oslo, formerly called Christiana, the capital of Norway, was founded in the eleventh century. It was the northernmost point reached during the cruise,

Around the World at Seventeen

and the sickening heat of the tropics was replaced by a frosty breath coming from the snow-mantled mountains. Here the sun set at 8:30 p.m.

We drove to Holmenkollen, high in the mountains, where we were to witness a contest of ski-jumping. As we passed out of the city into the country, we encountered snow in isolated patches, growing gradually heavier, until we were in a land of white, with the snow on the mountainsides ten feet and more deep. To most of us ski-jumping was no novelty; after the contest was over we repaired to the ski museum, where every possible type of ski is exhibited, including those worn by many famous jumpers. The exploration kit of Roald Amundsen is found here, with the garments he and his men wore, and kayaks, tents and dog sleds—even one of Amundsen's huskies is stuffed and sits there dreaming of the Northland. After our return from Holmenkollen we visited the building that housed the Oseberg ship. This ancient Viking vessel is believed to have belonged to Queen Asa, mother of King Hafdan the Black, who lived in the ninth century. It is a "femtansessa"—a boat rowed by thirty men—approximately sixty-nine feet long by seventeen wide. At the time it was dug up, the remains of two women were found in the ship together with many valuable relics which we later saw in the National Museum.

On the second day Fridtjof Nansen, the arctic

Around the World at Seventeen

explorer, gave the cruise a lecture on his explorations. A program followed in the assembly hall of the University of Oslo where we listened to the old Norse ballads and Norse school songs. The entertainment was climaxed by the native children singing the Stars and Stripes in excellent English. Then we put behind us the Land of the Midnight Sun and the *Ryndam* steamed out of the Oslofjord for Leith, England.

CHAPTER THIRTY

AFTER two days at sea we cruisers had our first view of the British Isles as the *Ryndam* steamed slowly up the picturesque Firth of Forth, past the highlands and moors of Scotland, with here and there an ancient baronial castle perched high on the hills overlooking the sea.

It did seem we had developed a mania for arriving at ports on Sundays, and Leith was no exception. Situated two miles from Edinburgh, it is connected with the latter by Leith Walk, practically a continuous street. Along this wide thoroughfare, Dessa Skinner and I taxied to Edinburgh. The weather was cold and a smoky haze enveloped us. Rosy-cheeked urchins played in the streets but few other people were abroad. In a few minutes we drew up at the junction of Prince Street and Leith Walk, the arrangement of the buildings here reminding me very much of the intersection of Fifth Avenue and Broadway, New York, in the neighborhood of the Flatiron Building. We breakfasted at a little restaurant and I had my first tilt with blue laws prevalent both in Scotland and England. I was told I could not smoke my pipe in the breakfast room.

But there was no law against smoking in a taxi

Around the World at Seventeen

and into one of these we hastily climbed. I was impatient to reach London, yet I was duty bound to at least gain a fleeting glimpse of the main points of interest in and around historic Edinburgh. Accordingly we dashed up the hill to Holyrood Castle, where memories of Mary, Queen of Scots, are brought to mind at every turn. A hurried trip through the court room, a pause at a window to view the Firth of Forth, and back again to the taxi. I judged from the expression on our cabby's face, he had never seen tourists show such speed. Edinburgh Castle was disposed of in a like manner and we passed by the home of the great John Knox with only a passing glance. A pause for lunch at "Ye Old Tavern"; a drive through the business district, and to the Station Hotel, where we spent the remainder of the afternoon browsing through Sunday editions.

At seven o'clock, we baggaged ourselves off to the depot. The train to Melrose was scheduled to depart at nine o'clock. We found the ticket window closed and the station empty. I pounded on the window loud enough to wake the dead. Finally, a gruff voice demanded to know what we wanted. Tickets, of course. Did we not know tickets were not sold on Sunday? More blue laws; we were forced to buy our tickets from the conductor when we boarded the train.

Somewhere I had gained the impression that Mel-

Around the World at Seventeen

rose was a town of size, an impression which was dispelled on our disembarking at a tiny deserted station at one end of an equally tiny and deserted street. I later learned the population numbered eighty-one. There we were with our grips in hand, no lights or signs to direct us to a night's lodging. We wandered up the street, finally meeting a pedestrian who helped us out of our predicament by directing us to the Abbey Hotel. Finding our way there we managed to arouse mine hostess and arranged for a room and breakfast. To alleviate the discomforts of cold, damp bedding, our hostess, who, by the way, possessed the ample proportions and beaming countenance always associated with one's idea of tavern keepers, furnished us with hot water bottles and hot bricks and soon we were lost in sleep.

When I awakened the next morning, I looked around for Skinner and found him at the window convulsed with laughter and mumbling to himself. He was reading the names on tombstones in an ancient graveyard just under our window, whereupon the virtues of departed housewives and the honesty of the husbandmen were extolled in glowing terms. The ruins of Melrose Abbey lay at the far side of the graveyard, picturesque and clear-cut in the early morning light, surrounded by clipped hedges, and beyond lay the gleaming countryside.

After a breakfast of porridge, tea, and rolls, served

Around the World at Seventeen

by our hostess at what she considered an unearthly hour, seven o'clock, we started for Abbotsford. Passing through a countryside made picturesque by groves of noble trees and sloping, green meadows fenced with well-clipped hedges to prevent the ever-present contented, fat cattle from wandering afield, we arrived at the home of Sir Walter Scott.

We swept into the courtyard through an ancient trellised iron gate, to be met by an aged custodian, a very likeness of Harry Lauder, Scotch burr, gnarled walking cane, and all. He might have been one of Scott's characters recalled to life for the purpose of relating to the pilgrim who has come to pay homage to the Great Romancer the endless tales current about him.

What an added thrill these tales gave me, as I stood at the living-room window where Sir Walter Scott himself had often stood, and looked down on the River Tweed wandering through the valley! And again, "Sir Walter's verry own pipe, sir," and penknife, on the much used reading table at which he was wont to sit. The rooms are preserved much as Scott left them; a suit of clothes he had worn was kept for display, as were many relics and pictures priceless to collectors. In the library are volumes which if placed on sale would probably bring more than Scott earned during the whole of his lifetime. For two hours, with the old Scotch custodian at our elbows, we lost our-

Around the World at Seventeen

selves in the traditional past; and then we departed for Dryburg Abbey.

We paused on the way at the point known as Scott's View, where he was accustomed to pause for a magnificent panorama of the valley; here, too, on the day Scott was buried, his favorite saddle horse paused, in conformance with the custom of his master when living. On beyond the View, the road led us close to the country home of Field Marshal Haig, of World War fame.

Dryburg Abbey is the oldest in the chain of Scottish Abbeys. The graves are so ancient that names and dates are worn away from the stones. And here, railed in by an iron picket fence, was the last resting place of the immortal Scott.

But we tarried only a moment at Dryburg Abbey, hastening back to Melrose, where we flagged a train for Chester. Once the border town, Carlisle, was put behind, we were in England. Chester, Stratford-on-Avon, and Oxford alone stood between us and our goal, London.

Chester is in the heart of Quaint England. We arrived there at three o'clock, and put up at a tavern that has survived Washington Irving's day, gabled and gilded, with great smoke-colored beams overhead, the fireplace awaiting the yule log, and the tavern surrounded by an old Roman wall. The wall, we know, separated the tavern from a graveyard; it likewise afforded a goodly view of the town. And

Around the World at Seventeen

after a walk around the premises, we adjourned to the dining room, where we partook of an appetizing meal of veal and ham pot-pie, kept piping hot by the charcoal fire under the serving table before being served.

Concluding our visit to Abbotsford, we departed for Lemmington Spa. Our arrival there was followed by a bus ride through a rural England, with a wonderful view of Warwick Castle from the winding road, and on to Stratford-on-Avon. We first visited Anne Hathaway's Cottage, and then the birthplace of her immortal husband. In Shakespeare's home, penned on the walls and carved in the woodwork, were the names of famous men who had come to pay homage to the recognized master. In the library were folio and quarto editions, more priceless even than the old manuscripts in Abbotsford. We paid a shilling each to enter the Shakespeare premises, which are under government supervision. Millions have made pilgrimage to the shrine of the immortal English poet and dramatist and the government is more than recompensed for its expenditures in upkeep.

Skinner and I took a long walk to the home of John Harvard, the founder of Harvard University, and returned to the Shakespeare Hotel, where every room is named after the plays and characters of the author. Here, also, we found a complete library of Shakespeare's works.

Around the World at Seventeen

We caught the bus back to Lemmington Spa and boarded the local for Oxford arriving there at five p.m. Skinner arranged for his entrance as an undergraduate, then we wandered around the campus and through Trinity and Christ Colleges, with their vine-covered walls that resembled those of old abbeys. We did not meet a single student while in Oxford.

We put up at the Mitre Hotel, four centuries old and supposed to be the quaintest hostlery in all England. We were escorted up a ladder to our rooms and the furnishings, I might say, were interesting from the standpoint of age, rather than for their comfort.

At last we boarded the train for London and arrived at Paddington Station, hailed a taxi, and were driven through Hyde Park to the Strand Palace Hotel, on the Strand. After all, what can one have to say about London? Any endeavor on my part to recount in chronological order the events of the full six days I spent there, is futile. Suffice to say: "I came; I saw—and was conquered."

I was on my own in London, and I made no studied itineraries. Anywhere I happened to be, I looked about me for the things of interest. In this manner I became more than casually acquainted with Piccadilly Circus and the Strand. The Embankment, with its foggy half-lights and quaint characters and the famous Parliament House with the equally famous

Around the World at Seventeen

Big Ben clock, grew familiar through my strolls. I came to know Hyde Park and the Pall Mall. Trafalgar Square and Shaftesbury Street became equally familiar. Buckingham Palace, the Tower of London, Westminster Abbey, Whitehall, and Rotten Row, became my very own through repeated visits. Hitherto, I had stinted myself, refraining from making purchases, against the time I should reach London. Now, I haunted the shops, and not in vain. But my interest in London could never make me forget that it was our last port of call before sailing home.

So, on June 19, the 214th day of the cruise, I boarded the *Ryndam* for the last time at Greenwich Pier, on the famous Thames River. The University World Cruise was drawing to a close, with twelve days only, between us and our starting point, New York.

Those were twelve hectic days, what with winding up our examinations, getting our cruise affairs straight with the management, lining up our college credits, and packing our belongings for the final shore trip.

No matter how we differed in opinion as to the merits of the various ports and the degree of discomforts to which we were subjected at times, on one thing we were, student body and faculty, in accord —the pioneer University World Cruise was a success. While we were eager to reach home, just as any other

Around the World at Seventeen

body of students leaving the college campus at the close of a hard year's work, still deep in our hearts we regretted the breaking up of what had been for so many months a closely-knit body of students. We had passed through a unique experiment, the success of which, no doubt, will call for another university cruise. For, basically, the idea is sound; and it remains only for the leaders to work out a schedule more adapted to the changing conditions which are met with in every foreign country.

Therefore, when in the late afternoon, the *Ryndam* dropped anchor at the foot of the Statue of Liberty, there was no shouting or rejoicing. After a final banquet, we went quietly to our quarters, put the finishing touches on our packing, and stood later at the gangplank as the *Ryndam* nosed slowly alongside the Hoboken dock of the Holland America Line.

A rattle of chains, the gangway was lowered. Several hundred rather subdued Cruisers departed from the vessel that had been their home for eight months; and as each went his way, it was with the deep conviction that a similar term spent in any land university, coupled with the most intensive training, could not have given him the first hand knowledge of peoples, countries, and the arts that he had acquired on the University Afloat.

THE END